For Matthew

I hope this book and many more
bring you the same pleasures that
they have always brought to me
now and throughout your life.

Sandra

THE OXFORD
NURSERY RHYME
BOOK

THE OXFORD NURSERY RHYME BOOK

ASSEMBLED BY
IONA AND PETER OPIE

With additional illustrations by
JOAN HASSALL

LONDON
OXFORD UNIVERSITY PRESS
NEW YORK   TORONTO

Oxford University Press, Ely House, London W. 1

GLASGOW NEW YORK TORONTO MELBOURNE WELLINGTON
CAPE TOWN IBADAN NAIROBI DAR ES SALAAM LUSAKA ADDIS ABABA
DELHI BOMBAY CALCUTTA MADRAS KARACHI LAHORE DACCA
KUALA LUMPUR SINGAPORE HONG KONG TOKYO

ISBN 0 19 869112 2

© *Iona and Peter Opie 1955*

First edition 1955
Reprinted with corrections 1957, 1960, 1963, 1967, 1973, 1975

*Printed in Great Britain
at the University Press, Oxford
by Vivian Ridler
Printer to the University*

Preface

GATHERED here are 800 rhymes and ditties. They are the infant jingles, riddles, catches, tongue-trippers, baby games, toe names, maxims, alphabets, counting rhymes, prayers, and lullabies, with which generation after generation of mothers and nurses have attempted to please the youngest, and have, somehow, usually succeeded.

In a child's life there is a period when almost the whole extent of his literature is the nursery rhyme. It comes (as far as books are concerned) at the transitional stage between the picture book pure and simple, and the first story book. During this period one can sit a child on one's lap with a good illustrated nursery rhyme book before one, and read the rhymes and point to the pictures for half an hour on end. The nursery rhyme book is, in fact, the first book which the parent is actually able to *read* to the child without his attention flagging.

With some of the rhymes the child is probably already familiar. He has heard them sung, he may know their names, he may even be able to repeat odd phrases from them; and his inborn musical fancy responds, as did Cowley's, to the 'tinkling of the rime and the dance of the numbers'. But the child probably has not previously given the verses any meaning. Now, he looks at the pictures in the book in relation to the words being read. He begins to identify particular objects with particular rhymes, a goose with 'Goosey, goosey gander', a shepherdess with 'Little Bo-peep', a cat and a fiddle with 'Hey diddle diddle'. Eventually he understands their stories.

These rhymes are the happy heritage of oral tradition: yet there is no need to feel disability in having to assist one's memory with a rhyme book. For more than 200 years the transmission of nursery rhymes has been aided by print; and if—as appears from the Introduction to *Tommy Thumb's (Pretty) Song Book*—the full-time nurse in George II's reign needed help with Mother Goose's repertoire, the parent of the twentieth century may be readily excused: there are almost certainly more nursery rhymes alive in the language today than at any time in the past. Certainly the present collection is larger than any previous one.

Our idea is that by making a book of rhymes which is comprehensive, the reader is offered the fullest scope for picking and choosing as his own fancy or memory dictates. Deliberately we have sometimes given more than one version of a rhyme; and deliberately we have sometimes given versions different from the text rhymes appearing in our *Oxford Dictionary of Nursery Rhymes*. We have no desire to establish standard texts. Oral tradition recognizes no 'correct' versions: the only defensible version is how one knows it oneself.[1]

ARRANGEMENT OF THE RHYMES

For this book we have divided the rhymes into nine sections. The accepted corpus of nursery song and jingle not only contains verse of very varying quality, but verses sometimes belonging to particular occasions, sometimes associated with particular actions, and sometimes, we think it will be seen, belonging to different stages of juvenile development. It has been our care that the rhymes should be shown to their best advantage, and we hope that our sectional arrangement, in which like is grouped with like, will add to the pleasure and usefulness of the collection.

It will be found that the baby games and lullabies of the first section belong, for the most part, to the period before a child is old enough to be read to. It contains the verses which a mother croons to her infant in his cot, and the baby-play, knee rides, and sayings for undressing, washing, and going to bed, which, in truth, are not a joy to repeat with book in hand. Our feeling is that a mother may

---

[1] There are, indeed, rhymes here which are not in the Dictionary. The present volume benefits from a further four years' collecting and from further kind correspondents who have added to our store. Quite a few rhymes and versions of rhymes assembled here, some of much beauty, have not hitherto been seen in print. Acknowledgements to contributors will appear in the next edition of the parent work. In the meantime further additions and variations, if possible with their pedigrees, will continue to be welcome at any time. Our eventual aim is to make a repository of all types of traditional verse.

like to look at this section when on her own, perhaps even before the child is born, so that she may have a rhyme in her mind ready for the demands of the particular querulous, damp, or twilight moment.

Most of the 'First Favourites' in the succeeding section will already be well known to every parent. Long usage has singled them out as the most memorable; and they have the simple Humpty Dumpty, jiggety joggety, alliterative and onomatopoeic appeal which finds immediate response with the very young. It is with these rhymes that lap reading usually begins.

'Little Songs' are gathered together in the third section, since to be able to sing, or to recognize a tune, seems to be a slightly later accomplishment. They are pieces, nevertheless, which 'may be either said or sung' (as the eighteenth-century editors were quick to point out), and the unmusical mother may also take comfort from the psychologists who aver that it does not matter to the child whether or not she is able to sing in tune. The fact delighted in is the special performance for the strictly limited audience. A mother's own voice is worth more than four-and-twenty professional singers trilling on the radio.

In the next section 'People' the rhymes evoke definite pictures, and to enjoy these cameos fully the child may want to understand the meanings of the words being repeated to him. This applies, also, to the fifth section 'A Little Learning' in which a child can, if he chooses, start acquiring schoolroom knowledge. Nobody, let it be said, would claim that alphabet and number rhymes enlarge a child's understanding of letters and figures, but, as a Scottish educationalist has pointed out, such rhymes do help to give a child a 'pleasurable attitude' to these first school subjects.

With our sixth section 'Awakening' a new, almost adult tone begins to pervade the verse. Here, perhaps, is the first hint of poetry, a hint according with the awakening senses which arise in many a child's breast earlier than is sometimes suspected. In this section a child may appreciate the feel of words as well as their meaning:

How many miles to Babylon?
Three-score and ten.
Can I get there by candle-light?
Yes, and back again.
If your heels are nimble and light,
You may get there by candle-light.

As Walter de la Mare has remarked, rhymes such as this 'free the fancy, charm tongue and ear, delight the inward eye', and can lead the way to poetry itself.

We continue along this special path in the seventh section 'Wonders' which advances into, perhaps, still more interesting country. This is a section of fancies and frolics, of lunacy and yet logic. There are examples of 'the self-evident proposition', beloved by our forefathers, and still a source of pleasure to youthful philosophers:

> There was a little guinea-pig
> Who, being little, was not big;

and there are revelations of the mind-magic of the word 'if': 'If all the trees were one tree . . . and the great man took the great axe, and cut down the great tree, and let it fall into the great sea, *what a splish-splash that would be!'*

The poetic view of life is maintained, too, in the section of riddles. Here, common objects are to be found dressed in the apparel of other objects. Ostensibly they have been so dressed for puzzlement, but the choice of costume has been the poet's. One has only to remember how the teeth are likened to thirty white horses stamping and champing on a red hill, and the way a snowflake is seen as a featherless white bird flying down from paradise, to realize that it is not merely sentiment which keeps these rhymes fresh.

Lastly come the ballads and more mature songs whose appeal may not be felt until the child has lit his seventh or eighth candle. The short and simple rhymes which were his constant delight when he was an apron-clinger may by now have been rejected; indeed, one may find all verse being set aside, and he will only listen to a story. Possibly he has already learned to read, and he crosses the seas with Robinson Crusoe, chuckles sympathetically with Doctor Dolittle, and learns something of mystery from Mrs. Molesworth. Verse seems to him too static, almost infantine. The response to metre which one thought one perceived in him at an earlier age seems entirely to have disappeared, and one wonders (or this is our experience) whether it was ever genuine. Yet, one day, perhaps stuck for something to read, he chances upon one of the longer and more exciting nursery ballads, such as 'The Derby Ram':

> Now the man that fed the ram, sir,
> He fed him twice a day,
> And each time that he fed him, sir,
> He ate a rick of hay.

He finds his interest caught. He finds the verse rollicking along, and things happening and a story being told more quickly, and arousing more laughter in less words than ever is possible in prose. He will be off again on another round of fun and music, and this second enjoyment of verse may be one without end. Such, anyway, is the story behind our arrangement of this collection; and the illustrations follow the same plan.

THE ILLUSTRATIONS

WHEN reading to our children we have repeatedly found that a rhyme in a nursery rhyme book is uninteresting to a small child (indeed, it is disregarded) unless it is accompanied by an illustration. The child looks at the sea of print and says 'Nothing on that page', meaning that there are no pictures on that page, and he turns over until he comes to a picture, and then wants to hear only the single rhyme which happens to be illustrated. This is something which John Newbery (1713–67), first and greatest of regular children's book publishers, understood very well. He, and his step-son Thomas Carnan, rarely printed a rhyme unless it was accompanied by some appropriate little woodcut. An illustration for a child, as they were well aware, need not be large, nor should it attempt to out-do the text; in fact it is an advantage if it is a simple statement matching the verse. However much a child's eye may momentarily be caught by a large flush of colour, there is a particular pleasure in examining and re-examining the precise miniature world of the Bewick-style engraving. There is little to be gained, we have found, from devoting a full-page coloured illustration to the first verse of 'Old Mother Hubbard' if the rest of the verses are left unillustrated. However ready a small child may be to like the complete story of 'Old Mother Hubbard' (we put it among the first in the lap-reading stage), he cannot go on looking at the one picture endlessly. He is read the first verse and sees the dog, the dame, and the empty cupboard; but when the second verse is read, he asks, 'Where is the bread and the dog which is dead?' and as it is not to be seen, his attention wanders. So it is that in the three primary sections for reading to the child (sections II, III, and IV) as many verses as possible, in fact almost every one, has its own illustration. In other sections other needs have been considered. In the first section, which is principally for the parent, illustrations to individual rhymes are few, except where it was felt that diagrammatic assistance might be appreciated. Again,

ix

in the last section, that for the more mature child, some of the songs are beyond precise visual interpretation, and what seemed to be called for were evocative headpieces in the manner of the old ballad sheets. In a song such as 'I saw a ship a-sailing, a-sailing on the sea' in which the vessel is manned by mice, commanded by a duck with a packet (some say a 'jacket') on his back, it is to our mind preferable to have the ship still in the distance, than to stunt the imagination with some exact interpretation of this curious phenomenon. Yet even in this section, as in sections VI and VII, precise detail has been admitted where it will add to the fun, and the diminishing muster of the 'Ten Little Injuns', and the increasing munificence of the gifts presented during 'The Twelve Days of Christmas', may be confirmed by the mathematically minded.

The majority of the illustrations are from chapbooks and toy books of the eighteenth and early nineteenth centuries, a period when wood engraving was brought to its zenith in the work of Thomas Bewick (1753–1828). Several of Bewick's engravings, as well as some by his brother John, will be recognized in these pages. Quite a few of the illustrations are those which originally accompanied the rhymes when they first appeared in print; and the design on page 3, which introduces our collection, is almost certainly the same as the one which illustrated the first rhyme in the first nursery rhyme book, published in 1744. Contemporary details of design and costume will be noted by the discerning; and such points as the date '1805' on Cock Robin's coffin (the date when the block was cut), and the eatable size of the pig which Tom, the piper's son, stole (the early accounts show that it was a pastry pig) will, we trust, add to the interest.[1]

In Joan Hassall, R.E., we have had the ideal collaborator. It is not only that she is recognized to be one of the finest wood engravers of our time, but her art was born out of the very chapbook literature she now accompanies. Her deep knowledge of the period of this style of illustration, her appreciation of juvenile lore and literature, and her sympathy with our aims, have been such that we were, so it seemed, collaborators in this work before ever we met. Initially her task was to illustrate those rhymes which never appeared in the early juvenile literature, or of which no satisfactory woodcut impression remains, but her wholeheartedness in this work has been such that her felicitous hand on the scraper board can be seen on

[1] A list of the sources of the illustrations will be found on p. 211.

eighty pages, including the nine fine section headings. Two years of close collaboration have been, for us, ones of mounting admiration for the grace and integrity of a remarkable craftswoman.[1]

The majority of the early illustrations have been drawn from the chapbook and juvenile literature in our own collection, but we could not have succeeded with our own resources alone and we are greatly indebted for permission to draw upon the collections in the British Museum, the Bodleian Library, the London Library, and, not least, upon Joan Hassall's own choice collection. We are, too, indebted to the Secretary of the Saltire Society for permission to use some of the nursery rhyme woodblocks which Joan Hassall engraved between 1943 and 1951 for the Society's series of *Saltire Chapbooks*; to Mr. C. E. Harris of Messrs. Francis Edwards for presenting us with W. S. Johnson's *Nursery Rhymes, c.* 1830; and to Mr. J. A. Birkbeck for the loan of nineteenth-century printers' ornaments.

A nursery rhyme book, naturally, stands or falls on whether it gives delight to the nursery; but, as we have already remarked, the handling of a nursery rhyme book, and the passing on of nursery rhymes, devolves upon the adult. Our hope is that nursery rhymes will continue, as they always have been, to be passed on in the home, and our endeavour has been to produce a book which, while pleasing the young, will not be entirely without friends amongst senior members of the family.

I. O. & P. O.

Alton in Hampshire
1955

[1] Some of the decorative problems have been far from straightforward. For instance, in the illustration of 'Old Mother Hubbard' three chapbook cuts were lacking, and Joan Hassall was given a commission similar to the one Ruskin gave Kate Greenaway when he induced her to illustrate additional verses to *Dame Wiggins of Lee*. Joan Hassall's skill in making good the 120-year-old deficiency may be measured on pp. 28–30.

Contents

BIRTHDAYS

MONDAY's child is fair of face,
Tuesday's child is full of grace,
Wednesday's child is full of woe,
Thursday's child has far to go,
Friday's child is loving and giving,
Saturday's child works hard for a living,
And the child that is born on the Sabbath day
Is bonny and blithe, and good and gay.

BABY GAMES
AND LULLABIES

To show the Features

Bo peeper,
Nose dreeper,
Chin chopper,
White lopper,
Red rag,
And little gap.

TAE titly,
Little fitty,
Shin sharpy,
Knee knapy,
Hinchie pinchy,
Wymie bulgy,
Breast berry,
Chin cherry,
Moo merry,
Nose nappy,
Ee winky,
Broo brinky,
Ower the croon,
And awa' wi' it.

EYE winker,
Tom tinker,
Nose smeller,
Mouth eater,
Chin chopper,
Guzzlewopper.

HEAD bumper,
Eyebrow branky,
Nose anky,
Mouth eater,
Chin chopper,
Gully, gully, gully.

BROW, brow, brenty,
Ee, ee, winky,
Nose, nose, nebbie,
Cheek, cheek, cherry,
Mou', mou', merrie,
Chin, chin, chackie,
Catch a flea, catch a flea.

TOE, trip and go,
Heel, tread a bank,
Shin, shinny shank,
Knee, knick a knack,
Thigh, thick a thack,
Tummy, trouble us,
    trouble us.

RING the bell, (*tug a lock of hair*)
Knock at the door, (*tap forehead*)
Peep in, (*peer into eyes*)
Lift the latch, (*tilt nose*)
Walk in, (*open mouth*)
Go way down cellar
    and eat apples. (*tickle throat*)

KNOCK at the doorie,
Peep in,
Lift the sneckie,
Clean yir feeties,
An' walk in.

HERE sits the Lord Mayor, (*forehead*)
    Here sit his men, (*eyes*)
Here sits the cockadoodle, (*right cheek*)
    Here sits the hen, (*left cheek*)
Here sit the little chickens, (*teeth*)
Here they run in, (*mouth*)
Chin chopper, chin chopper,
    Chin chopper, chin. (*chuck under chin*)

3

Five  Fingers

Thumb bold,
Thibity-thold,
Langman,
Lick pan,
Mammie's wee man.

Thumb he,
Wizbee,
Long Man,
Cherry Tree,
Little Jack-a-Dandy.

Tom Thumbkin,
Willie Wilkin,
Long Daniel,
Betty Bodkin,
And Little Dick.

FINGER DANCE

Dance, Thumbkin, dance,
Dance, Thumbkin, dance;
Dance, ye merry men, every one:
But Thumbkin, he can dance alone,
Thumbkin, he can dance alone.

Dance, Ringman, dance,
Dance, Ringman, dance;
Dance, ye merry men, every one:
But Ringman, he can dance alone,
Ringman, he can dance alone.

Dance, Foreman, dance,
Dance, Foreman, dance;
Dance, ye merry men, every one:
But Foreman, he can dance alone,
Foreman, he can dance alone.

Dance, Littleman, dance,
Dance, Littleman, dance;
Dance, ye merry men, every one:
But Littleman, he can dance alone,
Littleman, he can dance alone.

Dance, Longman, dance,
Dance, Longman, dance;
Dance, ye merry men, every one:
But Longman, he can dance alone,
Longman, he can dance alone.

Or: Thumbkin says, I'll dance,
Thumbkin says, I'll sing;
Dance and sing, you merry little men,
Thumbkin says, I'll dance and sing.
(And so on)

Thumbikin, Thumbikin, broke the barn,
Pinnikin, Pinnikin, stole the corn,
Long back'd Gray carried it away,
Old Mid-man sat and saw,
But Peesy-weesy paid for a'.

Five  Toes

Tommy Tibule,	Little Pig,	Toe Tipe,
Harry Wibule,	Pillimore,	Penny Wipe,
Tommy Tissle,	Grimithistle,	Tommy Thistle,
Harry Whistle,	Pennywhistle,	Billy Whistle,
Little Wee-wee-wee.	Great big Thumbo, father of them all.	Tripping-go.

This pig got in the barn,
This ate all the corn,
This said he wasn't well,
This said he'd go and tell,
And this said—weke, weke, weke,
I can't get over the barn door sill.

Let's go to the wood, says this pig,
What to do there? says that pig,
To look for my mother, says this pig,
What to do with her? says that pig,
Kiss her to death, says this pig.

This little pig had a rub-a-dub,
This little pig had a scrub-a-scrub,
This little pig-a-wig ran upstairs,
This little pig-a-wig called out, Bears!
Down came the jar with a loud
    Slam! Slam!
And this little pig had all the jam.

This little pig went to market,
This little pig stayed at home,
This little pig had roast beef,
This little pig had none,
And this little pig cried, Wee-wee-
    wee-wee-wee,
    I can't find my way home.

See-saw, Margery Daw,
The old hen flew over the malt house;
She counted her chickens one by one,
Still she missed the little white one,
And this is it, this is it, this is it.

The pettitoes are little feet,
    And the little feet not big;
Great feet belong to the grunting hog,
    And the pettitoes to the little pig.

Baby Play

Robert Barnes, fellow fine,
Can you shoe this horse of mine?
Yes, good sir, that I can,
As well as any other man.
There's a nail and there's a prod,
And now, good sir, your horse is
      shod.

Shoe a little horse,
Shoe a little mare,
But let the little colt
Go bare, bare, bare.

Shoe the colt, shoe the colt,
Shoe the wild mare.
Put a sack on her back,
See if she'll bear.
If she'll bear,
We'll give her some hay;
If she won't,
We'll send her away.

John Smith, fellow fine,
Can you shoe this horse of mine?
Yes I can, and that I can,
As well as any other man.
Put a nail upon his toe,
That's to make him trot and go.
Put a nail upon his sole,
That's to make him pay the toll.
Put a nail upon his heel,
That's to make him pace weel, pace
      weel, pace weel.

Is John Smith within?
Yes, that he is.
Can he set a shoe?
Aye, marry, two;
Here a nail and there a nail,
Tick, tack, too.

Hob, shoe, hob; hob, shoe, hob;
Here a nail, and there a nail,
And that's well shod.

The man in the mune
   is making shune,
Tuppence a pair an'
   they're a' dune.

Foot Games: Why infants should like having the soles of their feet patted they alone know. These rhymes, and the illustrations which accompanied them in the eighteenth century, show that it has long been so, particularly when the patting affects to be the hammering of a blacksmith.

ROUND about there
Sat a little hare,
The bow-wows came and chased
    him
    Right up there!

ROUND about, round about,
Catch a wee mouse;
Up a bit, up a bit,
In a wee house.

APPLE-PIE, apple-pie,
Peter likes apple-pie;
So do I, so do I.

TICKLY, tickly, on your knee,
If you laugh you don't love me.

IF you are a gentleman,
As I suppose you be,
You'll neither laugh nor smile
At the tickling of your knee.

ROUND about, round about, here sits
    the hare,
In the corner of a cornfield and that's
    just there.
    (*Close to thumb*)
This little dog found her,
This little dog ran her,
This little dog caught her,
This little dog ate her,
And this little dog said, Give me a
    little bit please.
    (*Fingers, starting with the thumb*)

ROUND and round the garden
Like a teddy bear;
One step, two step,
Tickle you under there!

FROM here to there
To Washington Square;
When I get there
I'll pull your hair.

AN old maid, an old maid,
You will surely be,
If you laugh or if you smile
While I tickle round your knee.

TICKLING GAMES: In the 'Round and round' and 'Round about' rhymes, circles are traced around the child's palm, and the steps or chases are conducted up the arm, ending with a prod in the arm-pit. In 'Apple-pie, apple-pie' two fingers are made to stride along the arm and over the crown of the head to the chin. The knee-cap 'neither laugh nor smile' games are also known in versions played on the hand. One attraction of tickling games is that after a while the child can choose to be the performer rather than the performed upon.

Here is the church, and here is the steeple;
Open the door and here are the people.
Here is the parson going upstairs,
And here he is a-saying his prayers.

The hands are interlocked back to back and bent round so that the palms face each other, the knuckles forming the ridge of the church roof. The little fingers are raised to form the steeple, the thumbs parted to open the door, and the hands turned inside out revealing a congregation of digits. To make the parson 'go upstairs' the hands are crossed back to back, and the fingers linked one by one. Still holding on, the palms are then brought together and the thumb appears in a pulpit of knotted hands.

Here are the lady's knives and forks,
Here is the lady's table,
Here is the lady's looking-glass,
And here is the baby's cradle.

Starting with the hands back to back, the fingers are interlaced to represent knives and forks. The hands are then turned over, the backs of the fingers forming the table. The little fingers are raised to make a looking-glass, and when the two forefingers are raised as well the hands are rocked like a cradle. 'Father Francis', below, is traditionally enacted with the two hands draped in handkerchiefs, or with shadows on the wall.

Good morning, Father Francis.
Good morning, Mrs. Sheckleton.
What has brought you abroad so early, Mrs. Sheckleton?
I have come to confess a great sin, Father Francis.
What is it, Mrs. Sheckleton?
Your cat stole a pound of my butter, Father Francis.
O, no sin at all, Mrs. Sheckleton.
But I killed your cat for it, Father Francis.
O, a very great sin indeed, Mrs. Sheckleton, you must do penance.
What penance, Father Francis?
Kiss me three times.
Oh! but I can't!
Oh! but you must!
Oh! but I can't!
Oh! but you must!
Well, what must be must,
So kiss, kiss, kiss, and away.

Deceptions · Marvels ·+·+·+·

HANDY dandy
Riddledy ro,
Which hand will you have,
High or low?

NIEVIE nievie nick nack,
Which hand will ye tak',
The richt or the wrang?
I'll beguile ye if I can.

Two little dicky birds,
Sitting on a wall;
One named Peter,
The other named Paul.
Fly away, Peter!
Fly away, Paul!
Come back, Peter!
Come back, Paul!

PUT your finger in Foxy's hole,
Foxy's not at home;
Foxy's at the back door,
Picking a marrow bone.

The sleight of hand in which two pieces of stamp paper, representing the dicky birds, are stuck on the backs of the forefingers and 'fly away' when the middle fingers are substituted, can mystify even seven-year-olds. But Foxy catches only the very innocent. The best type of Foxy's hole is made between the middle fingers, the hands forming a mound. When the child puts his finger in the hole, Foxy has come home again, and nips the intruder with the lurking thumb-nails. The hole, of course, remains open to allow escape.

MY father was a Frenchman,
A Frenchman, a Frenchman,
My father was a Frenchman
And he bought me a fiddle.
    He cut it here,
    He cut it there,
He cut it through the middle.

PEASE porridge hot,
Pease porridge cold,
Pease porridge in the pot
Nine days old.
Some like it hot,
Some like it cold,
Some like it in the pot
Nine days old.

BO-PEEP,
Little Bo-peep,
Now's the time for hide and seek.

DINGLE dingle doosey,
    The cat's in the well,
The dog's away to Bellingen
    To buy the bairn a bell.

The Frenchman's Fiddle is the child's arm, which is 'cut' above and below the elbow joint, and breaks in two when 'cut' in the middle. The Pease Porridge is represented by a pile of everybody's hands, and while each line is recited the hand at the bottom of the pile is pulled out and placed on the top. A Dingle Doosey is a stick from the fire, glowing at one end, which is whirled around so that it seems to make a red circle.

Dandling

Hey, my kitten, my kitten,
  And hey my kitten, my deary,
Such a sweet pet as this
  There is not far nor neary.
Here we go up, up, up,
  Here we go down, down, downy;
Here we go backwards and for-
    wards,
And here we go round, round,
    roundy.

See-saw, down in my lap,
  Up again onto her feet;
Little girl lost her white cap,
  Blown away in the street.

Dance a baby diddy,
What can mammy do wid 'e,
  But sit in her lap,
  And give 'un some pap,
And dance a baby diddy?

Smile, my baby bonny,
What will time bring on 'e?
  Sorrow and care,
  Frowns and grey hair,
So smile, my baby bonny.

Laugh, my baby beauty,
What will time do to ye?
  Furrow your cheek,
  Wrinkle your neck,
So laugh, my baby beauty.

Dance, my baby deary,
Mother will never be weary;
  Frolic and play,
  Now while you may,
So dance, my baby deary.

Dance, little baby, dance up high:
Never mind, baby, mother is by;
Crow and caper, caper and crow,
There, little baby, there you go;
Up to the ceiling, down to the
    ground,
Backwards and forwards, round and
    round:
Dance, little baby, and mother shall
    sing,
With the merry gay coral, ding,
    ding-a-ding, ding.

Catch him, crow! Carry him, kite!
Take him away till the apples are
    ripe;
When they are ripe and ready to fall,
Here comes baby, apples and all.

  Come dance a jig
    To my granny's pig,
  With a randy, rowdy, dowdy;
    Come dance a jig
    To my granny's pig,
  And pussy cat shall crowdy.

Hey diddle diddle,
    And hey diddle dan!
And with a little money,
    I bought an old man.
His legs were all crooked
    And wrongways set on,
So what do you think
    Of my little old man?

Hush, my baby, do not cry,
Papa's coming by and by;
When he comes he'll come in a gig,
Hi cockalorum, jig, jig, jig.

Dance to your daddy,
    My little babby,
Dance to your daddy,
    My little lamb.

Clap hands, clap hands,
    Till father comes home;
For father's got money,
    But mother's got none.

You shall have a fishy
    In a little dishy,
You shall have a fishy
    When the boat comes in.

Bring Daddy home
    With a fiddle and a drum,
A pocket full of spices,
    An apple and a plum.

You shall have an apple,
    You shall have a plum,
You shall have a rattle-basket
    When your daddy comes home.

In Scotland

Clap hands, Daddy comes
With his pocket full of plums,
    And a cake for *Johnny*.

Dance to your daddie,
    My bonnie laddie,
Dance to your daddie,
    My bonnie lamb.
And ye'll get a coatie,
    And a pair o' breekies—
Ye'll get a whippie
    And a supple Tam!

Clap hands, Daddy's coming
    Up the waggon way,
His pockets full of money
    And his hands full of clay.

How many days has my baby to play?
Saturday, Sunday, Monday,
Tuesday, Wednesday, Thursday, Friday,
Saturday, Sunday, Monday.
Hop away, skip away,
My baby wants to play;
My baby wants to play every day.

Knee Rides

Hɪᴇ to the market, Jenny come trot,
Spilt all her butter milk, every drop.
Every drop and every dram,
Jenny came home with an empty can.

Gᴇᴇ up, Neddy, to the fair;
What shall we buy when we get
    there?
A penny apple and a penny pear;
Gee up, Neddy, to the fair.

Dᴏɴᴋᴇʏ, Donkey, do not bray,
Mend your pace and trot away;
Indeed, the market's almost done,
My butter's melting in the sun.

A ʀᴏʙɪɴ and a robin's son
Once went to town to buy a bun.
They couldn't decide on plum or
    plain,
And so they went back home again.

Cᴏᴍᴇ up, my horse, to Budleigh Fair;
What shall we have when we get
    there?
Sugar and figs and elecampane;
Home again, home again, master
    and dame.

To market, to market,
    To buy a plum bun;
Home again, home again,
    Market is done.

To market, to market,
    To buy a fat pig,
Home again, home again,
    Jiggety-jig.
To market, to market,
    To buy a fat hog,
Home again, home again,
    Jiggety-jog.

Uᴘᴏɴ a cock-horse to market I'll
    trot,
To buy a pig to boil in the pot.
A shilling a quarter, a crown a side.
If it had not been killed, it would
    surely have died.

Fʀᴏᴍ Wibbleton to Wobbleton is
    fifteen miles,
From Wobbleton to Wibbleton is
    fifteen miles,
From Wibbleton to Wobbleton,
From Wobbleton to Wibbleton,
From Wibbleton to Wobbleton is
    fifteen miles.

12

TRIT trot to market to buy a penny
    doll;
Trit trot back again, the market's
    sold them all.

RIDE a cock-horse to Banbury Cross,
To buy little Johnny a galloping horse;
It trots behind and it ambles before,
And Johnny shall ride till he can ride
    no more.

RIDE away, ride away,
  Johnny shall ride,
He shall have a pussy cat
  Tied to one side;
He shall have a little dog
  Tied to the other,
And Johnny shall ride
  To see his grandmother.

RICHARD Dick upon a stick,
  Sampson on a sow,
We'll ride away to Colley Fair
  To buy a horse to plough.

CRIPPLE Dick upon a stick,
  Sandy on a soo,
Ride away to Galloway
  To buy a pound o' woo'.

THE MISCHIEVOUS RAVEN

A FARMER went trotting upon his grey mare,
    Bumpety, bumpety, bump!
With his daughter behind him so rosy and fair,
    Lumpety, lumpety, lump!

A raven cried, Croak! and they all tumbled down,
    Bumpety, bumpety, bump!
The mare broke her knees and the farmer his crown,
    Lumpety, lumpety, lump!

The mischievous raven flew laughing away,
    Bumpety, bumpety, bump!
And vowed he would serve them the same the next day,
    Lumpety, lumpety, lump!

13

More Knee Rides

This is the way the ladies ride,
  Nim, nim, nim, nim.
This is the way the gentlemen ride,
  Trim, trim, trim, trim.
This is the way the farmers ride,
  Trot, trot, trot, trot.
This is the way the huntsmen ride,
  A-gallop, a-gallop, a-gallop, a-gallop.
This is the way the ploughboys ride,
  Hobble-dy-gee, hobble-dy-gee.

Sometimes adding

  And when they come to a hedge—they jump over!
  And when they come to a slippery place—they scramble, scramble,
                    Tumble-down Dick!

CHICK! my naggie,
Chick! my naggie,
How many miles to
  Aberdaigy?
Eight and eight, and
  other eight,
Try to win there by
  candle light.

A TROT, and a canter, a gallop, and over,
Out of the saddle, and roll in the clover.

RIGADOON, rigadoon, now let him fly,
Sit him on father's foot, jump him up high.

LEG over leg,
  As the dog went to Dover,
When he came to a stile,
  Jump—he went over.

OLD Farmer Giles,
  He went seven miles
With his faithful dog Old Rover;
  And Old Farmer Giles,
    When he came to the stiles,
Took a run, and jumped clean over.

HERE comes my lady with her little baby,
  A nim, a nim, a nim.
Here comes my lord with his trusty sword,
  A trot, a trot, a trot.
Here comes old Jack with a broken pack,
  A gallop, a gallop, a gallop.

14

Ring Dances

Ring-a-ring o' roses,
A pocket full of posies,
 A-tishoo! A-tishoo!
We all fall down.

The cows are in the meadow
Lying fast asleep,
 A-tishoo! A-tishoo!
We all get up again.

Or this way

A ring, a ring o' roses,
A pocket full of posies,
 Ash-a! Ash-a!
All stand still.

The king has sent his daughter
To fetch a pail of water,
 Ash-a! Ash-a!
All bow down.

The bird upon the steeple
Sits high above the people,
 Ash-a! Ash-a!
All kneel down.

The wedding bells are ringing,
The boys and girls are singing,
 Ash-a! Ash-a!
All fall down.

Or

Round about the rosebush,
 Three steps,
 Four steps,
All the little boys and girls
 Are sitting
 On the doorsteps.

Sally go round the sun,
Sally go round the moon,
Sally go round the chimney-pots
On a Saturday afternoon.

Here we go dancing jingo-ring,
 Jingo-ring, jingo-ring,
Here we go dancing jingo-ring,
 About the merry-ma-tanzie.

Here we go round ring by ring,
 As ladies do in Yorkshire,
A curtsey here, a curtsey there,
 And a curtsey to the ground, sir.

Red stockings, blue stockings,
Shoes tied up with silver;
A red rosette upon my breast
And a gold ring on my finger.

So here we go around, around,
And here we go around;
Here we go around, around,
Till our skirts shall touch the ground.

15

'Skin a rabbit'

DIDDLE, diddle, dumpling, my son John,
Went to bed with his trousers on;
One shoe off, and one shoe on,
Diddle, diddle, dumpling, my son John.

FOOT PLAY

THE doggies went to the mill,
This way and that way;
They took a lick out of this one's sack,
They took a lick out of that one's sack,
And a leap in the stream, and a dip
    in the dam,
And went walloping, walloping,
    walloping home.

THIS is Willy Walker, and that's
    Tam Sim,
He ca'd him to a feast and he ca'd
    him;
And he sticket him wi' the spit, and
    he sticket him,
And he owre him, and he owre him,
And he owre him . . .
    Till day brak.

Go to bed first,
A golden purse;
Go to bed second,
A golden pheasant;
Go to bed third,
A golden bird.

DOWN with the lambs,
   Up with the lark,
Run to bed children
   Before it gets dark.

PUTTING ON NIGHTGOWN

LITTLE man in coal pit
   Goes knock, knock, knock;
Up he comes, up he comes,
   Out at the top.

FOOT PLAY

WAG a leg, wag a leg,
   Wag a leg along;
One mile to Auburton,
   Two miles to Tong.

FINGER NAILS

Cut them on Monday, you cut them for health;
Cut them on Tuesday, you cut them for wealth;
Cut them on Wednesday, you cut them for news;
Cut them on Thursday, a new pair of shoes;
Cut them on Friday, you cut them for sorrow;
Cut them on Saturday, see your true-love tomorrow;
Cut them on Sunday, you cut them for evil,
For all the next week you'll be ruled by the devil.

'Up the wooden hill'

Up the wooden hill
    to Bedfordshire,
Down Sheet Lane
    to Blanket Fair.

THREE A-BED

He that lies at the stock,
Shall have a gold rock;
He that lies at the wall,
Shall have a gold ball;
He that lies in the middle,
Shall have a gold fiddle.

Good night, God bless you,
Go to bed and undress you.

Good night, sweet repose,
Half the bed and all the clothes.

    Go to bed, Tom,
    Go to bed, Tom,
    Tired or not, Tom,
    Go to bed, Tom.

Now I lay me down to sleep,
I pray the Lord my soul to keep;
And if I die before I wake,
I pray the Lord my soul to take.

Matthew, Mark, Luke, and John,
Bless the bed that I lie on.
    Four corners to my bed,
    Four angels round my head;
    One to watch and one to pray
    And two to bear my soul away.

God bless this house from thatch to
    floor,
The twelve apostles guard the door
Four angels to my bed;
Gabriel stands at the head,
John and Peter at my feet,
All to watch me while I sleep.

    I see the moon,
        And the moon sees me;
    God bless the moon,
        And God bless me.

Moon, moon,
Mak' me a pair o' shoon,
And I'll dance till you be done.

Star light, star bright,
First star I see tonight,
I wish I may, I wish I might,
Have the wish I wish tonight.

Sing Lullaby

Hush-a-bye, baby, on the tree top,
When the wind blows the cradle will
    rock;
When the bough breaks the cradle
    will fall,
Down will come baby, cradle, and
    all.

Hush thee, my babby,
    Lie still with thy daddy,
Thy mammy has gone to the mill,
    To grind thee some wheat
    To make thee some meat,
So hush-a-bye, babby, lie still.

Hush-a-bye a baa lamb,
Hush-a-bye a milk cow,
We'll find a little stick
To beat the barking bow-wow.

I'll buy you a tartan bonnet,
And feathers to put upon it,
With a hush-a-bye and a lullaby,
Because you are so like your daddy.

Rock-a-bye, baby,
    Thy cradle is green,
Father's a nobleman,
    Mother's a queen;
And Betty's a lady,
    And wears a gold ring;
And Johnny's a drummer,
    And drums for the king.

Hush-a-bye, baby,
    The beggar shan't have 'ee,
No more shall the maggotty-pie;[1]
    The rooks nor the ravens
    Shan't carry 'ee to heaven,
So hush-a-bye, baby, bye-bye.

Hush-a-baa, baby,
    Dinna mak' a din,
An' ye'll get a cakie
    When the baker comes in.

Hush, little baby, don't say a word,
Papa's going to buy you a mocking bird.

If the mocking bird won't sing,
Papa's going to buy you a diamond ring.

If the diamond ring turns to brass,
Papa's going to buy you a looking-glass.

If the looking-glass gets broke,
Papa's going to buy you a billy-goat.

If that billy-goat runs away,
Papa's going to buy you another today.

[1] magpie.

18

THE little lady lairdie
She longed for a baby-o,
She took her father's greyhound
  And rowed it in a plaidie-o,
Saying, Hishie, bishie, bow, wow,
  Long legs hast thou,
If it wasn't for your cold nose
  I would kiss thee now-o.

BYE, baby bunting,
Daddy's gone a-hunting,
Gone to get a rabbit skin
To wrap the baby bunting in.

HUSHIE ba, burdie beeton,
Your Mammie's gone to Seaton,
For to buy a lammie's skin
To wrap your bonnie boukie in.

HUSH-A-BYE, baby, they're gone to
  milk,
Lady and milkmaid all in silk,
Lady goes softly, maid goes slow,
Round again, round again, round
  they go.

BYE, bye, baby bunting,
Your Daddy's gone a-hunting,
Your Mammy's gone the other way,
To beg a jug of sour whey
For little baby bunting.

FATHER's gone a-flailing,
Brother's gone a-nailing,
Mother's gone a-leasing,
Granny's come a-pleasing,
Sister's gone to Llantwit Fair,
Baby, baby, will go there.

HUSH-A-BA birdie, croon, croon,
Hush-a-ba birdie, croon,
The sheep are gane to the silver wood,
And the cows are gane to the broom, broom.

And it's braw milking the kye, kye,
It's braw milking the kye,
The birds are singing, the bells are ringing,
The wild deer come galloping by, by.

And hush-a-ba birdie, croon, croon,
Hush-a-ba birdie, croon,
The gaits are gane to the mountain hie,
And they'll no be hame till noon, noon.

Encore till the child's asleep

Baby, baby, naughty baby,
Hush, you squalling thing, I say.
Peace this moment, peace, or maybe
Bonaparte will pass this way.

Baby, baby, he's a giant,
Tall and black as Rouen steeple,
And he breakfasts, dines, rely on't,
Every day on naughty people.

Baby, baby, if he hears you,
As he gallops past the house,
Limb from limb at once he'll tear you,
Just as pussy tears a mouse.

And he'll beat you, beat you, beat you,
And he'll beat you all to pap,
And he'll eat you, eat you, eat you,
Every morsel snap, snap, snap.

FIRST
FAVOURITES

A a B

GREAT A, little a,
   Bouncing B,
The cat's in the cupboard
And can't see me.

HEY diddle, diddle,
   The cat and the fiddle,
The cow jumped over the moon;
   The little dog laughed
   To see such sport,
And the dish ran away with
      the spoon.

PAT-A-CAKE, pat-a-cake, baker's man,
Bake me a cake as fast as you can;
Pat it and prick it, and mark it
   with T,
Put it in the oven for Tommy and
   me.

ICKLE ockle, blue bockle,
   Fishes in the sea,
If you want a pretty maid,
   Please choose me.

Bow-wow, says the dog,
Mew, mew, says the cat,
Grunt, grunt, goes the hog,
And squeak goes the rat.
Tu-whu, says the owl,
Caw, caw, says the crow,
Quack, quack, says the duck,
And what cuckoos say you know.

NAUTY Pauty Jack-a-Dandy
Stole a piece of sugar candy
From the grocer's shoppy-shop,
And away did hoppy-hop.

Jingles

HIGGLETY, pigglety, pop!
The dog has eaten the mop;
  The pig's in a hurry,
  The cat's in a flurry,
Higglety, pigglety, pop!

HICKORY, dickory, dock,
The mouse ran up the clock.
  The clock struck one,
  The mouse ran down,
Hickory, dickory, dock.

HOKEY, pokey, whisky, thum,
How d'you like potatoes done?
Boiled in whisky, boiled in rum,
Says the King of the Cannibal
    Islands.

HODDLEY, poddley, puddle and fogs,
Cats are to marry the poodle dogs;
Cats in blue jackets and dogs in red
    hats,
What will become of the mice and
    the rats?

JEREMIAH, blow the fire,
  Puff, puff, puff!
First you blow it gently,
  Then you blow it rough.

Jingles

Humpty Dumpty sat on a wall,
Humpty Dumpty had a great fall;
All the King's horses and all the King's
    men
Couldn't put Humpty together again.

Hey diddle dinkety, poppety, pet,
The merchants of London they wear
    scarlet;
Silk in the collar and gold in the hem,
So merrily march the merchant men.

Jack be nimble,
    Jack be quick,
Jack jump over
    The candlestick.

Rub-a-dub-dub,
    Three men in a tub,
And how do you think they got there?
    The butcher, the baker,
    The candlestick-maker,
    They all jumped out of a rotten
        potato,
'Twas enough to make a man stare.

Little fishes in a brook,
Father caught them on a hook,
Mother fried them in a pan,
Johnnie eats them like a man.

Hark, Hark

HARK, hark,
The dogs do bark,
The beggars are coming to town;
Some in rags,
And some in jags,
And one in a velvet gown.

IN LINCOLN LANE

I LOST my mare in Lincoln Lane,
I'll never find her there again;
She lost a shoe,
And then lost two,
And threw her rider in the drain.

TIT, TAT, TOE

TIT, tat, toe,
My first go,
Three jolly butcher boys
All in a row;
Stick one up, stick one down,
Stick one in the old man's crown.

FATHER GREYBEARD

OLD Father Greybeard
Without tooth or tongue,
If you'll give me your finger
I'll give you my thumb.

GOOSEY GANDER

GOOSEY, goosey gander,
Whither shall I wander?
Upstairs and downstairs
And in my lady's chamber.
There I met an old man
Who would not say his prayers,
I took him by the left leg
And threw him down the stairs.

BATTLE ROYAL

THE lion and the unicorn
Were fighting for the crown;
The lion beat the unicorn
All around the town.

Some gave them white bread,
And some gave them brown;
Some gave them plum cake
And drummed them out of town.

Ding, Dong, Bell

Ding, dong, bell,
Pussy's in the well.
Who put her in?
Little Johnny Green.
Who pulled her out?
Little Tommy Stout.
What a naughty boy was that
To try to drown poor pussy cat,
Who never did him any harm,
And killed the mice in his father's
      barn.

A Scottish Version

Ding dang, bell rang,
Cattie's in the well, man.
Fa' dang her in, man?
Jean and Sandy Din, man.
Fa' took her oot, man?
Me and Willie Cout, man.
A' them that kent her
      When she was alive,
Come to the burialie
      Between four and five.

TOM TITTLEMOUSE

Little Tom Tittlemouse
Lived in a bell-house;
The bell-house broke,
And Tom Tittlemouse woke.

TOMMY TITTLEMOUSE

Little Tommy Tittlemouse
Lived in a little house;
He caught fishes
In other men's ditches.

HINX, MINX

Hinx, minx, the old witch winks,
The fat begins to fry,
Nobody at home but Jumping Joan,
Father, Mother, and I.
Stick, stock, stone dead,
Blind man can't see;
Every knave will have a slave,
You or I must be he.

CONTRARY MARY

Mary, Mary, quite contrary,
      How does your garden grow?
With silver bells and cockle shells,
      And pretty maids all in a row.

27

THE COMIC ADVENTURES OF

Old Mother Hubbard and Her Dog

OLD Mother Hubbard
Went to the cupboard,
To fetch her poor dog a bone;
But when she got there
The cupboard was bare
And so the poor dog had none.

She went to the baker's
To buy him some bread;
But when she came back
The poor dog was dead.

She went to the undertaker's
To buy him a coffin;
But when she came back
The poor dog was laughing.

She took a clean dish
To get him some tripe;
But when she came back
He was smoking a pipe.

She went to the fishmonger's
   To buy him some fish;
But when she came back
   He was licking the dish.

She went to the tavern
   For white wine and red;
But when she came back
   The dog stood on his head.

She went to the fruiterer's
   To buy him some fruit;
But when she came back
   He was playing the flute.

She went to the tailor's
   To buy him a coat;
But when she came back
   He was riding a goat.

She went to the hatter's
   To buy him a hat;
But when she came back
   He was feeding the cat.

OLD MOTHER HUBBARD
Continued

She went to the barber's
  To buy him a wig;
But when she came back
  He was dancing a jig.

She went to the cobbler's
  To buy him some shoes;
But when she came back
  He was reading the news.

She went to the seamstress
  To buy him some linen;
But when she came back
  The dog was a-spinning.

She went to the hosier's
  To buy him some hose;
But when she came back
  He was dressed in his clothes.

The dame made a curtsey,
  The dog made a bow;
The dame said, Your servant,
  The dog said, Bow-wow.

SING JIGMIJOLE

Sing jigmijole, the pudding bowl,
The table and the frame;
My master he did cudgel me,
For kissing of my dame.

SOLOMON GRUNDY

Solomon Grundy,
Born on a Monday,
Christened on Tuesday,
Married on Wednesday,
Took ill on Thursday,
Worse on Friday,
Died on Saturday,
Buried on Sunday.
This is the end
Of Solomon Grundy.

PUSSY CAT

Pussy cat ate the dumplings,
Pussy cat ate the dumplings,
Mamma stood by,
And cried, Oh, fie!
Why did you eat the dumplings?

GIFT FOR THE QUEEN

Pretty maid, pretty maid,
Where have you been?
Gathering roses
To give to the Queen.
Pretty maid, pretty maid,
What gave she you?
She gave me a diamond,
As big as my shoe.

SQUABBLES

My little old man and I fell out,
How shall we bring this matter
about?
Bring it about as well as you can,
And get you gone, you little old
man!

Moll-in-the-wad and I fell out,
What do you think it was all about?
I gave her a shilling, she swore it
was bad,
It's an old soldier's button, says
Moll-in-the-Wad.

The Queen
of
Hearts

THE Queen of Hearts
She made some tarts,
All on a summer's day;
The Knave of Hearts
He stole those tarts,
And took them clean away.

The King of Hearts
Called for the tarts,
And beat the knave full sore;
The Knave of Hearts
Brought back the tarts,
And vowed he'd steal no more.

COBBLER, COBBLER

COBBLER, cobbler, mend my shoe,
Get it done by half past two;
Stitch it up, and stitch it down,
Then I'll give you half a crown.

LITTLE TEE-WEE

LITTLE Tee-wee,
He went to sea,
In an open boat;
And when it was afloat,
The little boat bended.
My story's ended.

CHARLEY

CHARLEY, Charley,
Stole the barley
Out of the baker's shop.
The baker came out
And gave him a clout,
Which made poor Charley hop.

The Girl
in
the Lane

The girl in the lane,
That couldn't speak plain,
   Cried, Gobble, gobble, gobble.
The man on the hill,
That couldn't stand still,
   Went hobble, hobble, hobble.

LITTLE NAG

I HAD a little nag
   That trotted up and down;
I bridled him, and saddled him,
   And trotted out of town.

THE CROOKED MAN

There was a crooked man,
   And he walked a crooked mile,
He found a crooked sixpence
   Against a crooked stile;
He bought a crooked cat,
   Which caught a crooked mouse,
And they all lived together
   In a little crooked house.

TOMMY AND BESSY

As Tommy Snooks and Bessy
   Brooks
   Were walking out one Sunday,
Says Tommy Snooks to Bessy
   Brooks,
   Tomorrow will be Monday.

KINDNESS

If I had a donkey that wouldn't go,
Would I beat him? Oh no, no.
I'd put him in the barn and give him some corn,
The best little donkey that ever was born.

BLUE BELL

I HAD a little dog and his name was
    Blue Bell,
I gave him some work, and he did it
    very well;
I sent him upstairs to pick up a pin,
He stepped in the coal-scuttle up to
    his chin;
I sent him to the garden to pick
    some sage,
He tumbled down and fell in a rage;
I sent him to the cellar to draw a pot
    of beer,
He came up again and said there was
    none there.

BUFF

I HAD a dog
    Whose name was Buff,
I sent him for
    A bag of snuff;
He broke the bag
    And spilt the stuff,
And that was all
    My penny's worth.

TWO LITTLE DOGS

Two little dogs
Sat by the fire
Over a fender of coal-dust;
    Said one little dog
    To the other little dog,
If you don't talk, why, I must.

BY THE FIRE

PUSSY sits beside the fire,
    So pretty and so fair.
In walks the little dog,
    Ah, pussy, are you there?
How do you do, Mistress Pussy?
    Mistress Pussy, how do you do?
I thank you kindly, little dog,
    I'm very well just now.

KINDNESS

I LOVE little pussy,
    Her coat is so warm,
And if I don't hurt her
    She'll do me no harm.
So I'll not pull her tail,
    Nor drive her away,
But pussy and I
    Very gently will play.
She shall sit by my side,
    And I'll give her some food;
And pussy will love me
    Because I am good.

34

and Pussy Cats ·······

VISITOR

Who's that ringing at my door bell?
  A little pussy cat that isn't very well.
Rub its little nose with a little mutton fat,
  That's the best cure for a little pussy cat.

WEDDING

Pussicat, wussicat, with a white foot,
When is your wedding and I'll come to it.
The beer's to brew, and the bread's to bake,
Pussicat, wussicat, don't be too late.

PUSS UP THE PLUM TREE

Diddlety, diddlety, dumpty,
The cat ran up the plum tree;
Half a crown to fetch her down,
Diddlety, diddlety, dumpty.

A TRAVELLER

Pussy cat, pussy cat,
  Where have you been?
I've been to London
  To look at the Queen.
Pussy cat, pussy cat,
  What did you there?
I frightened a little mouse
  Under her chair.

A SCOTTISH CAT

Poussie, poussie, baudrons,
  Where hae ye been?
I've been to London,
  Seeing the Queen.
Poussie, poussie, baudrons,
  What got ye there?
I got a guid fat mousikie,
  Rinning up a stair.
Poussie, poussie, baudrons,
  What did ye do wi't?
I put it in my meal-poke,
  To eat it to my bread.

PUSS IN THE PANTRY

Hie, hie, says Anthony,
Puss is in the pantry,
Gnawing, gnawing,
  A mutton, mutton bone;
See how she tumbles it,
See how she mumbles it,
See how she tosses
  The mutton, mutton bone.

Mary's Lamb

And so the teacher turned it out,
  But still it lingered near,
And waited patiently about
  Till Mary did appear.

MARY had a little lamb,
  Its fleece was white as snow;
And everywhere that Mary went
  The lamb was sure to go.

It followed her to school one day,
  That was against the rule;
It made the children laugh and play
  To see a lamb at school.

Why does the lamb love Mary so?
  The eager children cry;
Why, Mary loves the lamb, you
  know,
  The teacher did reply.

BETTY PRINGLE'S PIG

LITTLE Betty Pringle she had a pig,
It was not very little and not very
  big;
When it was alive it lived in clover,
But now it's dead and that's all over.
Johnny Pringle he sat down and cried,
Betty Pringle she lay down and died;
So there was an end of one, two,
  three,
Johnny Pringle he, Betty Pringle she,
  And Piggy Wiggy.

ROBIN HOOD

ROBIN Hood
Has gone to the wood;
He'll come back again
If we are good.

THE STAR

TWINKLE, twinkle, little star,
How I wonder what you are!
Up above the world so high,
Like a diamond in the sky.

WILLIE WINKIE

WEE Willie Winkie runs through the town,
Upstairs and downstairs in his night-gown,
Rapping at the window, crying through the lock,
Are the children all in bed, for now it's eight o'clock?

Polly Flinders

Little Polly Flinders
Sat among the cinders,
Warming her pretty little toes;
Her mother came and caught her,
And whipped her little daughter
For spoiling her nice new clothes.

MRS. HEN

Chook, chook, chook, chook, chook,
  Good morning, Mrs. Hen.
How many chickens have you got?
  Madam, I've got ten.
Four of them are yellow,
  And four of them are brown,
And two of them are speckled red,
  The nicest in the town.

A FARTHING

I went into my
      grandmother's garden,
And there I found
      a farthing.
I went into my
      next door neighbour's;
There I bought
A pipkin and a popkin,
A slipkin and a slopkin,
A nailboard, a sailboard,
And all for a farthing.

THE LITTLE GIRL

There was a little girl, and she had a little curl
    Right in the middle of her forehead;
When she was good she was very, very good,
    But when she was bad she was horrid.

One day she went upstairs, while her parents, unawares,
    In the kitchen were occupied with meals;
And she stood upon her head, on her little truckle-bed,
    And then began hurraying with her heels.

Her mother heard the noise and thought it was the boys,
    A-kicking up a rumpus in the attic;
But when she climbed the stair, and saw Jemima there,
    She took her and did whip her most emphatic.

37

Georgie Porgie

GEORGIE Porgie, pudding and pie,
Kissed the girls and made them cry;
When the boys came out to play,
Georgie Porgie ran away.

TOMMY'S SHOP

TOMMY kept a chandler's shop,
Richard went to buy a mop;
Tommy gave him such a whop,
That sent him out of the chandler's
    shop.

PARLIAMENT SOLDIERS

HIGH diddle ding, did you hear the
    bells ring?
The parliament soldiers are gone to
    the king.
Some they did laugh, and some they
    did cry,
To see the parliament soldiers go by.

BUTTERFLY

I'M a little butterfly
    Born in a bower,
Christened in a teapot,
    Died in half an hour.

BOY BLUE

LITTLE Boy Blue,
    Come blow your horn,
The sheep's in the meadow,
    The cow's in the corn.

Where is the boy
    Who looks after the sheep?
He's under a haycock
    Fast asleep.
Will you wake him?
    No, not I,
For if I do,
    He's sure to cry.

SIX LITTLE MICE

SIX little mice sat down to spin;
Pussy passed by and she peeped in.
What are you doing, my little men?
Weaving coats for gentlemen.
Shall I come in and cut off your threads?
No, no, Mistress Pussy, you'd bite off
    our heads.
Oh, no, I'll not; I'll help you to spin.
That may be so, but you don't come in.

Miss Muffet

LITTLE Miss Muffet
  Sat on a tuffet,
Eating her curds and whey;
  There came a big spider,
  Who sat down beside her
And frightened Miss Muffet away.

JACK IN THE PULPIT

JACK in the pulpit, out and in,
Sold his wife for a minikin pin.

MY LITTLE MAID

HEY diddle dout,
  My candle's out,
My little maid's not at home;
  Saddle the hog,
  And bridle the dog,
And fetch my little maid home.

Home she came, trittity trot,
She asked for the porridge she left
    in the pot;
Some she ate, and some she shod,
And some she gave to the truckler's
    dog.

MY BLACK HEN

HICKETY, pickety, my black hen,
She lays eggs for gentlemen;
Gentlemen come every day
To see what my black hen doth lay.

THE FLYING PIG

DICKERY, dickery, dare,
The pig flew up in the air;
The man in brown
Soon brought him down,
Dickery, dickery, dare.

THREE YOUNG RATS

THREE young rats with black felt hats,
Three young ducks with white straw flats,
Three young dogs with curling tails,
Three young cats with demi-veils,
Went out to walk with two young pigs
In satin vests and sorrel wigs;
But suddenly it chanced to rain
And so they all went home again.

RIDE A COCK-HORSE

RIDE a cock-horse to Banbury Cross,
To see a fine lady upon a white
 horse;
Rings on her fingers and bells on her
 toes,
And she shall have music wherever
 she goes.

DAVY DUMPLING

DAVY Davy Dumpling,
 Boil him in the pot;
Sugar him and butter him,
 And eat him while he's hot.

FISHES SWIM

FISHES swim in water clear,
Birds fly up into the air,
Serpents creep along the ground,
Boys and girls run round and round.

THE DOVE SAYS

THE dove says, Coo, coo,
What shall I do?
I can scarce maintain two.
Pooh, pooh, says the wren,
I have ten,
And keep them all like gentlemen.

CURR dhoo, curr dhoo,
Love me, and I'll love you.

DUM AND DEE

TWEEDLEDUM and Tweedledee
 Agreed to have a battle,
For Tweedledum said Tweedledee
 Had spoiled his nice new rattle.
Just then flew by a monstrous crow
 As big as a tar-barrel,
Which frightened both the heroes so,
 They quite forgot their quarrel.

TOM TINKER'S DOG

Bow, wow, wow,
Whose dog art thou?
Little Tom Tinker's dog,
Bow, wow, wow.

RIDE A COCK-HORSE

RIDE a cock-horse
To Banbury Cross,
To see what Tommy can buy;
A penny white loaf,
A penny white cake,
And a two-penny apple pie.

LITTLE GENERAL MONK

COCK AND HEN

Hen: COCK, cock, cock, cock,
I've laid an egg,
Am I to go ba-are foot?

Cock: Hen, hen, hen, hen,
I've been up and down,
To every shop in town,
And cannot find a shoe
To fit your foot,
If I'd crow my hea-rt out.

FEATHERS

CACKLE, cackle, Mother Goose,
Have you any feathers loose?
Truly have I, pretty fellow,
Half enough to fill a pillow.
Here are quills, take one or two,
And down to make a bed for you.

LITTLE General Monk
Sat upon a trunk,
Eating a crust of bread;
There fell a hot coal
And burnt in his clothes a hole,
Now little General Monk is dead.

41

Jack and Jill

AND

OLD DAME DOB

JACK and Jill
Went up the hill,
To fetch a pail of water;
Jack fell down,
And broke his crown,
And Jill came tumbling after.

Then up Jack got,
And home did trot,
As fast as he could caper;
To old Dame Dob,
Who patched his nob
With vinegar and brown paper.

When Jill came in,
How she did grin
To see Jack's paper plaster;
Her mother, vexed,
Did whip her next,
For laughing at Jack's disaster.

Now Jack did laugh
And Jill did cry,
But her tears did soon abate;
Then Jill did say,
That they should play
At see-saw across the gate.

42

Simple Simon

AND

THE PIEMAN

~~~~~~~~~~~~~~~~~~~~~~~~~~~~~~~~~

SIMPLE Simon met a pieman,
  Going to the fair;
Says Simple Simon to the pieman,
  Let me taste your ware.

Says the pieman to Simple Simon,
  Show me first your penny;
Says Simple Simon to the pieman,
  Indeed I have not any.

Simple Simon went a-fishing,
  For to catch a whale;
All the water he had got
  Was in his mother's pail.

Simple Simon went to look
  If plums grew on a thistle;
He pricked his fingers very much,
  Which made poor Simon whistle.

He went for water in a sieve
  But soon it all fell through;
And now poor Simple Simon
  Bids you all adieu.

43

BAA, BAA, BLACK SHEEP

Baa, baa, black sheep,
　Have you any wool?
Yes, sir, yes, sir,
　Three bags full;
One for the master,
　And one for the dame,
And one for the little boy
　Who lives down the lane.

SAM, THE SPORTSMAN

There was a little man, and he had a little gun,
　And his bullets were made of lead, lead, lead;
He went to the brook, and shot a little duck,
　Right through the middle of the head, head, head.

He carried it home to his old wife Joan,
　And bade her a fire for to make, make, make,
To roast the little duck he had shot in the brook,
　And he'd go and fetch her the drake, drake, drake.

TOMMY TUCKER

Little Tommy Tucker
　Sings for his supper:
What shall we give him?
　White bread and butter.
How shall he cut it
　Without e'er a knife?
How will he be married
　Without e'er a wife?

JACK SPRAT'S CAT

Jack Sprat
Had a cat,
It had but one ear;
　It went to buy butter
When butter was dear.

44

A SCOTTISH SHOE

THERE was a wee bit wifie,
  Who lived in a shoe;
She had so many bairns,
  She kenn'd na what to do.
She gaed to the market
  To buy a sheep-head;
When she came back
  They were a' lying dead.
She went to the wright
  To get them a coffin;
When she came back
  They were a' lying
    laughing.
She gaed up the stair,
  To ring the bell;
The bell rope broke,
  And down she fell.

THE OLD WOMAN IN A SHOE

THERE was an old woman who lived in a shoe,
She had so many children she didn't know
    what to do;
She gave them some broth without any bread;
She whipped them all soundly and put them
    to bed.

JACK SPRAT

JACK Sprat could eat no fat,
  His wife could eat no lean,
And so between them both, you see,
  They licked the platter clean.

JACK SPRAT'S PIG

LITTLE Jack Sprat
  Once had a pig;
It was not very little,
  Nor yet very big,
It was not very lean,
  It was not very fat—
It's a good pig to grunt,
  Said little Jack Sprat.

JACK HORNER

LITTLE Jack Horner
Sat in the corner,
Eating a Christmas pie;
He put in his thumb,
And pulled out a plum,
And said, What a good boy am I!

Tom, the Piper's Son

Tom, Tom, the piper's son,
Stole a pig and away he run;
  The pig was eat,
  And Tom was beat,
And Tom went howling down the
    street.

Yes, yes, Tom stole the pig, and here's the man from whom he stole it.

This man makes pigs of pastry and fills their middles with currants, and places two little currants in their heads for eyes. When he walks in the street with his basket of pigs for sale, he cries: 'Who buys? Who buys?' and he sings:

A long-tailed pig,
  Or a short-tailed pig,
Or a pig without any tail;
  A sow pig,
  Or a boar pig,
Or a pig with a curly tail.
Take hold of the tail
  And eat off his head,
And then you'll be sure
  The pig-hog is dead.

While the man was selling a curly-tailed pig to a little Miss, Tom ran away with a long-tailed pig: but he would not have stolen it if he had known what sauce he would have to it.

For he was beat in the street, and made to beg pardon on his marrow-bones, and promise never to steal anything again. Thus after the sweetmeat of stealing he got the sour sauce of correction.

The House that Jack Built

THIS is the house
    that Jack built.

This is the malt
That lay in the house
    that Jack built.

This is the rat,
That ate the malt
That lay in the house
    that Jack built.

This is the cat,
That killed the rat,
That ate the malt
That lay in the house
    that Jack built.

This is the dog,
That worried the cat,
That killed the rat,
That ate the malt
That lay in the house
    that Jack built.

This is the cow with the crumpled horn,
That tossed the dog,
That worried the cat,
That killed the rat,
That ate the malt
That lay in the house
    that Jack built.

This is the maiden all forlorn,
That milked the cow with the crumpled horn,
That tossed the dog,
That worried the cat,
That killed the rat,
That ate the malt
That lay in the house
    that Jack built.

This is the man all tattered and torn,
That kissed the maiden all forlorn,
That milked the cow with the crumpled horn,
That tossed the dog,
That worried the cat,
That killed the rat,
That ate the malt
That lay in the house
    that Jack built.

This is the priest all shaven and shorn,
That married the man all tattered and torn,
That kissed the maiden all forlorn,
That milked the cow with
    the crumpled horn,
That tossed the dog,
That worried the cat,
That killed the rat,
That ate the malt
That lay in the house
    that Jack built.

48

This is the cock that crowed in the morn,
That waked the priest all shaven and shorn,
That married the man all tattered and torn,
That kissed the maiden all forlorn,
That milked the cow with the crumpled horn,
That tossed the dog,
That worried the cat,
That killed the rat,
That ate the malt
That lay in the house
that Jack built.

This is the farmer sowing his corn,
That kept the cock that crowed in the morn,
That waked the priest all shaven and shorn,
That married the man all tattered and torn,
That kissed the maiden all forlorn,
That milked the cow with the crumpled horn,
That tossed the dog,
That worried the cat,
That killed the rat,
That ate the malt
That lay in the house
that Jack built.

This is the horse and the hound and the horn,
That belonged to the farmer sowing his corn,
That kept the cock that crowed in the morn,
That waked the priest all shaven and shorn,
That married the man all tattered and torn,
That kissed the maiden all forlorn,
That milked the cow with the
crumpled horn,
That tossed the dog,
That worried the cat,
That killed the rat,
That ate the malt
That lay in the house
that Jack built.

49

Robinets and Jenny Wrens

PIT, PAT

Pit, pat, well-a-day,
Little Robin flew away;
Where can little Robin be?
Gone into the cherry tree.

FIDGET

As little Jenny Wren
  Was sitting by the shed,
She waggled with her tail,
  She nodded with her head;
She waggled with her tail,
  She nodded with her head,
As little Jenny Wren
  Was sitting by the shed.

COCK ROBIN'S COURTSHIP

Cock Robin got up early
  At the break of day,
And went to Jenny's window
  To sing a roundelay.
He sang Cock Robin's love
  To little Jenny Wren,
And when he got unto the end
  Then he began again.

UNGRATEFUL JENNY

Jenny Wren fell sick
  Upon a merry time,
In came Robin Redbreast
  And brought her sops and
    wine.

Eat well of the sop, Jenny,
  Drink well of the wine.
Thank you, Robin, kindly,
  You shall be mine.

BOB ROBIN

Little Bob Robin,
Where do you live?
Up in yonder wood, sir,
On a hazel twig.

Jenny Wren got well,
  And stood upon her feet;
And told Robin plainly,
  She loved him not a bit.

THE NORTH WIND

The north wind doth blow,
And we shall have snow,
And what will poor Robin do then?
  Poor thing.
He'll sit in a barn,
And keep himself warm,
And hide his head under his wing,
  Poor thing.

Robin he got angry,
  And hopped upon a twig,
Saying, Out upon you, fie
  upon you,
    Bold faced jig!

God Almighty's Cocks and Hens

LITTLE FRIEND

In the greenhouse lives a wren,
Little friend of little men;
When they're good she tells them
   where
To find the apple, quince, and pear.

GREED

The robin and the wren,
They fought upon the porridge pan;
But ere the robin got a spoon,
The wren had ate the porridge down.

VISITOR

Little Robin Redbreast
Came to visit me;
This is what he whistled,
Thank you for my tea.

NIDDLE NODDLE

Little Robin Redbreast
Sat upon a rail;
Niddle noddle went his head,
Wiggle waggle went his tail.

CATCH

Little Robin Redbreast sat upon a tree,
Up went pussy cat, and down went he;
Down came pussy, and away Robin ran;
Says little Robin Redbreast, Catch me if you can.
Little Robin Redbreast jumped upon a wall,
Pussy cat jumped after him, and almost got a fall;
Little Robin chirped and sang, and what did
   pussy say?
Pussy cat said, Mew, and Robin jumped away.

FOUR WRENS

There were two wrens upon a tree,
Whistle and I'll come to thee;
Another came, and there were three,
Whistle and I'll come to thee;
Another came and there were four,
You needn't whistle any more,
For being frightened, off they flew,
And there are none to show to you.

PRAISE

Robinets and Jenny Wrens
Are God Almighty's cocks and hens.
The martins and the swallows
Are God Almighty's bows and
   arrows.

WARNING

The robin and the redbreast,
The robin and the wren:
If you take from their nest
You'll never thrive again.

HEY DOROLOT

Hey, dorolot, dorolot!
  Hey, dorolay, dorolay!
Hey, my bonny boat, bonny boat,
  Hey, drag away, drag away!

JUMPING JOAN

Here am I,
  Little Jumping Joan;
When nobody's with me
  I'm all alone.

GRIG'S PIG

Grandfa' Grig
  Had a pig,
In a field of clover;
  Piggy died,
  Grandfa' cried,
And all the fun was over.

LITTLE BIRD

Once I saw a little bird
  Come hop, hop, hop,
And I cried, Little bird,
  Will you stop, stop, stop?

I was going to the window
  To say, How do you do?
But he shook his little tail
  And away he flew.

POLL PARROT

Little Poll Parrot
Sat in his garret
Eating toast and tea;
  A little brown mouse
  Jumped into the house,
And stole it all away.

WARM hands, warm,
  The men have gone to plough,
If you want to warm your hands,
  Warm your hands now.

Brush hair, brush,
  The men have gone to plough,
If you want to brush your hair,
  Brush your hair now.

Wash hands, wash,
  The men have gone to plough,
If you want to wash your hands,
  Wash your hands now.

PUSSY CAT MOLE

PUSSY cat Mole jumped over a coal
And in her best petticoat burnt a
  great hole.
Poor pussy's weeping, she'll have
  no more milk
Until her best petticoat's mended
  with silk.

Cock: LOCK the dairy door,
  Lock the dairy door!

Hen: Chickle, chackle, chee,
  I haven't got a key!

BED TIME

COME, let's to bed,
Says Sleepy-head;
Tarry a while, says Slow;
Put on the pot,
Says Greedy-gut,
We'll sup before we go.

ROUND ABOUT

ROUND about, round about,
  Maggotty pie;
My father loves good ale,
  And so do I.

53

WASH THE DISHES

WASH the dishes, wipe the dishes,
  Ring the bell for tea;
Three good wishes, three good
    kisses,
  I will give to thee.

TIDDLE LIDDLE

TIDDLE liddle lightum,
  Pitch and tar;
Tiddle liddle lightum,
  What's that for?

TEASING

LITTLE Jack Horner
  Sat in the corner,
Eating his curds and whey;
  There came a big spider,
  Who sat down beside her,
And the dish ran away with the spoon.

'Daddy, you haven't got it right!'

LITTLE SONGS

Sing a Song of Sixpence

Sɪɴɢ a song of sixpence,
  A pocket full of rye;
Four and twenty blackbirds,
  Baked in a pie.

When the pie was opened,
  The birds began to sing;
Was not that a dainty dish,
  To set before the king?

The king was in his counting-house,
  Counting out his money;
The queen was in the parlour,
  Eating bread and honey.

The maid was in the garden,
  Hanging out the clothes,
When down came a blackbird
  And pecked off her nose.

Happy ending:

  They sent for the king's doctor,
    Who sewed it on again,
  And he sewed it on so neatly,
    The seam was never seen.

BOYS AND GIRLS COME OUT TO PLAY

Boys and girls come out to play,
The moon doth shine as bright as day.
Leave your supper and leave your sleep,
And join your playfellows in the street.
Come with a whoop and come with a call,
Come with a good will or not at all.
Up the ladder and down the wall,
A half-penny loaf will serve us all;
You find milk, and I'll find flour,
And we'll have a pudding in half an hour.

A Scots version

LAZY deuks that sit i' the
    coal-neuks,
And winna come out to
    play;
Leave your supper, and
    leave your sleep,
Come out and play at
    hide-and-seek.

YANKEE DOODLE

YANKEE Doodle came to town,
    Riding on a pony;
He stuck a feather in his cap
    And called it macaroni.

SPIN DAME

SPIN, Dame, spin,
Your bread you must win;
Twist the thread and break it not,
Spin, Dame, spin.

RUMPTY-IDDITY, row, row, row,
If I had a good supper,
    I could eat it now.

MY MAID MARY

MY maid Mary,
    She minds the dairy,
While I go a-hoeing and mowing
    each morn;
    Merrily runs the reel,
    And the little spinning wheel,
Whilst I am singing and mowing
    my corn.

BLOW, WIND, BLOW

BLOW, wind, blow!
And go, mill, go!
That the miller may grind his corn;
That the baker may take it,
And into bread make it,
And bring us a loaf in the morn.

THE COACHMAN

UP at Piccadilly oh!
The coachman takes his stand,
And when he meets a pretty girl,
He takes her by the hand;
Whip away for ever oh!
Drive away so clever oh!
All the way to Bristol oh!
He drives her four-in-hand.

MY LITTLE COW

I HAD a little cow,
Hey diddle, ho diddle!
I had a little cow,
        and I drove it to the stall;
Hey diddle, ho diddle!
        and there's my song all.

JEMMY DAWSON

BRAVE news is come to town,
Brave news is carried;
Brave news is come to town,
Jemmy Dawson's married.

First he got a porridge-pot,
Then he bought a ladle;
Then he got a wife and child,
And then he bought a cradle.

A SONG

I'LL sing you a song,
Nine verses long,
    For a pin;
Three and three are six,
And three are nine;
You are a fool,
    And the pin is mine.

59

YOU SHALL BE QUEEN

LILIES are white,
  Rosemary's green,
When I am king,
  You shall be queen.

ROSES are red,
  Violets are blue,
Sugar is sweet
And so are you.

BIRD SCARER'S SONG

O ALL you little blackey
    tops,
Pray don't you eat my
    father's crops,
While I lie down to take
    a nap.
  Shua-O! Shua-O!

If father he perchance
    should come,
With his cocked hat and
    his long gun,
Then you must fly and I
    must run.
  Shua-O! Shua-O!

WASHING DAY

THE old woman must stand
  At the tub, tub, tub,
The dirty clothes
  To rub, rub, rub;
But when they are clean,
  And fit to be seen,
She'll dress like a lady,
  And dance on the green.

I'LL TELL

I'LL tell my own daddy,
  When he comes home,
What little good work
  My mammy has done;
She has earned a penny
  And spent a groat,
And burnt a hole
  In the child's new coat.

IPSEY WIPSEY

IPSEY Wipsey spider
  Climbing up the spout;
Down came the rain
  And washed the spider out:
Out came the sunshine
  And dried up all the rain;
Ipsey Wipsey spider
  Climbing up again.

FATHER SHORT

FATHER Short came down
    the lane;
Oh! I'm obliged to hammer
    and smite
From four in the morning
    till eight at night,
For a bad master, and a
    worse dame.

HEY DING A DING

HEY ding a ding,
    What shall I sing?
How many holes in a
    skimmer?
    Four-and-twenty.
    My plate's empty;
Pray, mamma, give us our
    dinner.

SING, SING

SING, sing,
    What shall I sing?
The cat's run away
    With the pudding string!
Do, do,
    What shall I do?
The cat's run away
    With the pudding too!

THE CUCKOO

THE cuckoo is a merry bird,
    She sings as she flies;
She brings us good tidings,
    And tells us no lies.

She sucks little birds' eggs
    To make her voice clear,
That she may sing Cuckoo!
    Three months in the year.

TEA-TIME

POLLY put the kettle on,
Polly put the kettle on,
Polly put the kettle on,
    We'll all have tea.

Sukey take it off again,
Sukey take it off again,
Sukey take it off again,
    They've all gone away.

Or

POLLY put the kettle on,
Sally blow the bellows strong,
Molly call the muffin man,
    We'll all have tea.

Jingle Bells

JINGLE, bells! jingle, bells!
Jingle all the way;
Oh, what fun it is to ride
In a one-horse open sleigh.

BAGPIPES

PUSS came dancing out of a barn
With a pair of bagpipes under her arm;
She could sing nothing but, Fiddle cum fee,
The mouse has married the humble-bee.
Pipe, cat—dance, mouse—
We'll have a wedding at our good house.

THE BRAVE
OLD DUKE OF YORK

OH, the brave old Duke of York,
He had ten thousand men;
He marched them up to the top of
the hill,
And he marched them down again.
And when they were up, they were up,
And when they were down, they
were down,
And when they were only half-way up,
They were neither up nor down.

AT BELLE ISLE

AT the siege of Belle Isle
I was there all the while—
All the while,
All the while,
At the siege of Belle Isle.

THE KING OF FRANCE

THE king of France, the king of France,
with forty thousand men,
Oh, they all went up the hill, and so—
they all came down again.

Old King Cole

OLD King Cole
Was a merry old soul,
And a merry old soul was he;
  He called for his pipe,
  And he called for his bowl,
And he called for his fiddlers three.

Every fiddler he had a fiddle,
And a very fine fiddle had he;
  Oh, there's none so rare
  As can compare
With King Cole and his fiddlers
    three.

BILLY AND ME

ONE, two, three,
I love coffee,
And Billy loves tea,
How good you be,
One, two, three,
I love coffee,
And Billy loves tea.

JIM CROW

TWIST about, turn about,
  Jump Jim Crow;
Every time I wheel about
  I do just so.

THE LEGACY

MY father died a month ago
  And left me all his riches;
A feather bed, a wooden leg,
  And a pair of leather breeches;
A coffee pot without a spout,
  A cup without a handle,
A tobacco pipe without a lid,
  And half a farthing candle.

THREE BLIND MICE

THREE blind mice, see how they run!
They all ran after the farmer's wife,
Who cut off their tails with a carving knife,
Did you ever see such a thing in your life,
  As three blind mice?

Little Bo-peep

Little Bo-peep has lost her sheep,
    And doesn't know where to find them;
Leave them alone, and they'll come home,
    Bringing their tails behind them.

Little Bo-peep fell fast asleep,
    And dreamt she heard them bleating;
But when she awoke, she found it a joke,
    For they were still a-fleeting.

Then up she took her little crook,
    Determined for to find them;
She found them indeed, but it made her heart bleed,
    For they'd left their tails behind them.

It happened one day, as Bo-peep did stray
    Into a meadow hard by,
There she espied their tails side by side,
    All hung on a tree to dry.

She heaved a sigh, and wiped her eye,
    And over the hillocks went rambling,
And tried what she could, as a shepherdess should,
    To tack again each to its lambkin.

The Three Little Kittens

THREE little kittens
They lost their mittens,
  And they began to cry,
Oh, mother dear,
We sadly fear
  Our mittens we have lost.
What! lost your mittens,
You naughty kittens!
  Then you shall have no pie.
  Mee-ow, mee-ow, mee-ow.
  No, you shall have no pie.

The three little kittens
Put on their mittens
  And soon ate up the pie;
Oh, mother dear,
We greatly fear
  Our mittens we have soiled.
What! soiled your mittens,
You naughty kittens!
  Then they began to sigh,
  Mee-ow, mee-ow, mee-ow,
  Then they began to sigh.

The three little kittens
They found their mittens,
  And they began to cry,
Oh, mother dear,
See here, see here,
  Our mittens we have found.
Put on your mittens,
You silly kittens,
  And you shall have some pie.
  Purr-r, purr-r, purr-r,
  Oh, let us have some pie.

The three little kittens
They washed their mittens,
  And hung them out to dry;
Oh! mother dear,
Do you not hear,
  Our mittens we have washed.
What! washed your mittens,
Then you're good kittens,
  But I smell a rat close by.
  Mee-ow, mee-ow,
    mee-ow,
  We smell a rat
    close by.

Country

WILLY BOY

WILLY boy, Willy boy,
   Where are you going?
I will go with you,
   If that I may.
I'm going to the meadow
   To see them a-mowing,
I am going to help them
   Turn the new hay.

BANBURY FAIR

As I was going to Banbury,
   Upon a summer's day,
My dame had butter, eggs, and fruit,
   And I had corn and hay.
Joe drove the ox, and Tom the swine,
   Dick took the foal and mare;
I sold them all—then home to dine,
   From famous Banbury fair.

THE OLD WOMAN'S THREE COWS

THERE was an old woman had three cows,
   Rosy and Colin and Dun.
Rosy and Colin were sold at the fair,
And Dun broke her heart in a fit of despair,
So there was an end of her three cows,
   Rosy and Colin and Dun.

66

Songs

AN OWL IN AN OAK

THERE was an owl lived in an oak,
　Wisky, wasky, weedle;
And every word he ever spoke
　Was, Fiddle, faddle, feedle.

A gunner chanced to come that way,
　Wisky, wasky, weedle;
Says he, I'll shoot you, silly bird.
　Fiddle, faddle, feedle.

WHOSE LITTLE PIGS

WHOSE little pigs are these, these, these?
　Whose little pigs are these?
They are Roger the Cook's, I know by their looks;
　I found them among my peas.
Go pound them, go pound them.
　I dare not on my life,
For though I love not Roger the Cook,
　I dearly love his wife.

Oranges and Lemons

GAY GO UP AND GAY GO DOWN,
TO RING THE BELLS OF LONDON TOWN.

Bull's eyes and targets,
Say the bells of St. Marg'ret's.

Brickbats and tiles,
Say the bells of St. Giles'.

Oranges and lemons,
Say the bells of St. Clement's.

Pancakes and fritters,
Say the bells of St. Peter's.

Two sticks and an apple,
Say the bells at Whitechapel.

Old Father Baldpate,
Say the slow bells at Aldgate.

Maids in white aprons,
Say the bells at St. Catherine's.

Pokers and tongs,
Say the bells at St. John's.

Kettles and pans,
Say the bells at St. Anne's.

You owe me five farthings,
Say the bells of St. Martin's.

When will you pay me?
Say the bells at Old Bailey.

When I grow rich,
Say the bells at Shoreditch.

Pray, when will that be?
Say the bells at Stepney.

I'm sure I don't know,
Says the great bell at Bow.

Here comes a candle to light you to bed,
Here comes a chopper to chop off your head.

68

NATURAL HISTORY

WHAT are little boys made of, made of?
What are little boys made of?
    Frogs and snails
    And puppy-dogs' tails,
That's what little boys are made of.

What are little girls made of, made of?
What are little girls made of?
    Sugar and spice
    And all things nice,
That's what little girls are made of.

What are young men made of, made of?
What are young men made of?
    Sighs and leers
    And crocodile tears,
That's what young men are made of.

What are young women made of, made of?
What are young women made of?
    Ribbons and laces
    And sweet pretty faces,
That's what young women are made of.

Cock a doodle doo

LUCY AND KITTY

Lucy Locket lost her pocket,
  Kitty Fisher found it;
Not a penny was there in it,
  Only ribbon round it.

COCK-CROW

THE cock's on the wood pile
  Blowing his horn,
The bull's in the barn
  A-threshing the corn,
The maids in the meadow
  Are making the hay,
The ducks in the river
  Are swimming away.

Cock a doodle doo!
My dame has lost her shoe,
My master's lost his fiddling stick,
And knows not what to do.

Cock a doodle doo!
What is my dame to do?
Till master finds his fiddling stick
She'll dance without her shoe.

Cock a doodle doo!
My dame has found her shoe,
And master's found his fiddling
    stick,
Sing doodle doodle doo.

Cock a doodle doo!
My dame will dance with you,
While master fiddles his fiddling
    stick
For dame and doodle doo.

WHERE IS HE?

OH where, oh where has my little
    dog gone?
  Oh where, oh where can he be?
With his ears cut short and his tail
    cut long,
  Oh where, oh where is he?

AN OLD WOMAN

THERE was an old woman tossed up in a basket,
  Seventeen times as high as the moon;
Where she was going I couldn't but ask it,
  For in her hand she carried a broom.
Old woman, old woman, old woman, quoth I,
Where are you going to up so high?
To brush the cobwebs off the sky!
May I go with you? Aye, by-and-by.

Dappled Grey

I HAD a little horse,
  His name was Dappled Grey,
His head was made of gingerbread,
  His tail was made of hay:
He could amble, he could trot,
  He could carry the mustard pot,
He could amble, he could trot,
  Through the old town of Windsor.

A SONG

I'LL sing you a song,
The days are long,
The woodcock and the sparrow;
The little dog has burnt his tail,
And he must be hanged tomorrow.

CHRISTMAS EVE

ON Christmas Eve I turned the spit,
I burnt my fingers, I feel it yet;
The little cock sparrow flew over
    the table,
The pot began to play with the ladle.

POP GOES THE WEASEL

UP and down the City Road,
  In and out the Eagle,
That's the way the money goes,
  Pop goes the weasel!

Half a pound of tuppenny rice,
  Half a pound of treacle,
Mix it up and make it nice,
  Pop goes the weasel!

Every night when I go out
  The monkey's on the table;
Take a stick and knock it off,
  Pop goes the weasel!

TWO BIRDS

THERE were two birds sat on a stone,
    Fa, la, la, la, lal, de;
One flew away, and then there was one,
    Fa, la, la, la, lal, de;
The other flew after, and then there was none,
    Fa, la, la, la, lal, de;
And so the poor stone was left all alone,
    Fa, la, la, la, lal, de.

Street Songs

THE TOY LAMB SELLER

GET ready your money and come to me,
I sell a young lamb for one penny.
Young lambs to sell! Young lambs to sell!
If I'd as much money as I could tell,
I never would cry, Young lambs to sell!

THE RABBIT MAN

HERE I am with my rabbits
    Hanging on my pole,
The finest Hampshire rabbits
    That e'er crept from a hole.

THE BROOM SQUIRE'S SONG

HERE's a large one for the lady,
Here's a small one for the baby;
Come buy, my pretty lady,
Come buy o' me a broom.

THE HOT PEASE MAN

PIPING hot, smoking hot,
What I've got, you have not.
Hot, hot pease, hot, hot, hot;
Hot are my pease, hot.

CHAIRS TO MEND

IF I'd as much money as I could spend,
I never would cry, Old chairs to mend.
Old chairs to mend! Old chairs to mend!
I never would cry, Old chairs to mend.

'BLACK YOUR HONOUR'S SHOES?'

HERE's Finiky Hawkes,
    As busy as any;
Will well black your shoes,
    And charge but a penny.

OLD CLOTHES, ANY OLD CLO', CLO'

If I'd as much money
As I could tell,
I never would cry,
Old clothes to sell!
Old clothes to sell!
Old clothes to sell!
I never would cry,
Old clothes to sell!

THE GINGERBREAD MAN

Smiling girls, rosy boys,
Come and buy my little toys;
Monkeys made of gingerbread,
And sugar horses painted red.

BUY ANY BUTTONS?

Buttons, a farthing a pair,
Come, who will buy them of me?
They are round and sound and pretty,
And fit for the girls of the city.
Come, who will buy them of me?
Buttons, a farthing a pair.

HOT CROSS BUNS

Hot cross buns! Hot cross buns!
One a penny, two a penny,
Hot cross buns!
If your daughters do not like them
Give them to your sons;
And if you have not any of these pretty little elves,
You cannot do better than eat them yourselves.

SWEET BLOOMING LAVENDER

Come all you young ladies and make no delay—
I gathered my lavender fresh from Mitcham today.

Will you buy my sweet blooming lavender?
There are sixteen dark blue branches a penny.

You buy it once you will buy it twice;
It will make your clothes smell sweet and nice.

Who'll buy my sweet blooming lavender?
Sixteen full branches a penny.

This song is still sung in the streets of London.

73

Charms and

TO THE CUCKOO

Cuckoo, cuckoo, what do you do?
In April I open my bill;
In May I sing all day;
In June I change my tune;
In July away I fly;
In August away I must.

TO THE MAGPIE

Magpie, magpie, flutter and flee,
Turn up your tail and good luck
    come to me.

One for sorrow, two for joy,
Three for a girl, four for a boy,
Five for silver, six for gold,
Seven for a secret ne'er to be told.

TO THE PUSS MOTH

Millery, millery, dustipole,
How many sacks have you stole?
Four and twenty and a peck,
Hang the miller by his neck.

TO THE LADYBIRD

Ladybird, ladybird,
  Fly away home,
Your house is on fire
  And your children all gone;
All except one
  And that's little Ann
And she has crept under
  The warming pan.

Bless you, bless you, burnie-bee,
Tell me when my wedding be;
If it be tomorrow day,
Take your wings and fly away.
Fly to the east, fly to the west,
Fly to him I love the best.

TO THE BAT

Bat, bat, come under my hat,
  And I'll give you a slice of
    bacon;
And when I bake, I'll give you
  a cake,
  If I am not mistaken.

Invocations

Rain, rain, go away,
Come again another day,
Little Johnny wants to play.

Rain, rain, go to Spain,
Never show your face again.

It's raining, it's pouring,
The old man's snoring;
He got into bed
And bumped his head
And couldn't get up in the
morning.

It's raining, it's raining,
There's pepper in the box,
And all the little ladies
Are picking up their frocks.

Rain on the green grass,
And rain on the tree,
Rain on the house-top,
But not on me.

MILKING

Cushy cow, bonny, let down thy
milk,
And I will give thee a gown of silk;
A gown of silk and a silver tee,
If thou wilt let down thy milk for me.

Snow, snow faster,
Ally-ally-blaster;
The old woman's plucking her geese,
Selling the feathers a penny a piece.

Snail, snail, put out your horns,
And I'll give you bread and barley
corns.

CHURNING

Come, butter, come,
Come, butter, come;
Peter stands at the gate
Waiting for a butter cake.
Come, butter, come.

LONDON BRIDGE

LONDON Bridge is broken down,
  Broken down, broken down,
London Bridge is broken down,
  My fair lady.

Build it up with wood and clay,
  Wood and clay, wood and clay,
Build it up with wood and clay,
  My fair lady.

Wood and clay will wash away,
  Wash away, wash away,
Wood and clay will wash away,
  My fair lady.

Build it up with bricks and mortar,
  Bricks and mortar, bricks and
    mortar,
Build it up with bricks and mortar,
  My fair lady.

Bricks and mortar will not stay,
  Will not stay, will not stay,
Bricks and mortar will not stay,
  My fair lady.

Build it up with iron and steel,
  Iron and steel, iron and steel,
Build it up with iron and steel,
  My fair lady.

Iron and steel will bend and bow,
  Bend and bow, bend and bow,
Iron and steel will bend and bow,
  My fair lady.

Build it up with silver and gold,
  Silver and gold, silver and gold,
Build it up with silver and gold,
  My fair lady.

Silver and gold will be stolen away,
  Stolen away, stolen away,
Silver and gold will be stolen away,
  My fair lady.

Set a man to watch all night,
  Watch all night, watch all night,
Set a man to watch all night,
  My fair lady.

Suppose the man should fall asleep,
  Fall asleep, fall asleep,
Suppose the man should fall asleep,
  My fair lady.

Give him a pipe to smoke all night,
  Smoke all night, smoke all night,
Give him a pipe to smoke all night,
  My fair lady.

Games for Small Toughs

TITTY cum tawtay,
  The ducks in the water:
Titty cum tawtay,
  The geese follow after.

MARCHING

MARCH, march, head erect,
Left, right, that's correct.

PICK-A-BACK

MATTHEW, Mark, Luke, and John,
Hold my horse till I leap on,
Hold him steady, hold him sure,
And I'll get over the misty moor.

RACE STARTING

BELL horses, bell horses,
  What time of day?
One o'clock, two o'clock,
  Three and away.

ONE to make ready,
  And two to prepare;
Good luck to the rider,
  And away goes the mare.

ONE for money,
  Two for show,
Three to make ready,
  And four to go.

SEE-SAW

SEE-SAW, Margery Daw,
Jacky shall have a new master;
Jacky shall have but a penny a day,
Because he can't work any faster.

SEE-SAW, Margery Daw,
Sold her bed and lay upon straw;
Was not she a dirty slut
To sell her bed and lie in the dirt.

KING OF THE CASTLE

I'M the king of the castle,
Get down you dirty rascal.

SCOTTISH CASTLE

I, WILLIE Wastle,
  Stand on my castle,
An' a' the dogs o' your toon,
Will no' drive Willie Wastle doon.

DUCKS AND DRAKES

A DUCK and a drake,
A nice barley-cake,
With a penny to pay the old baker;
A hop and a scotch
Is another notch,
Slitherum, slatherum, take her.

AMERICAN jump, American jump,
One—two—three.
Under the water, under the sea,
Catching fishes for my tea,
—Dead,
Or, Alive,
Or, Round the world?

The child holds the grown-up's hands and is jumped up and down to the first two lines. At 'three' the child has an extra big jump and twists his legs around the adult's waist. The child's body is then allowed to fall backwards until his head nearly touches the floor. He is asked 'Dead or alive or round the world'. If he chooses 'Dead' he is dropped on to the floor; if 'Alive' he is pulled upright; if, as is usual, he chooses 'Round the world', he is whirled round and round for as long as possible.

CHOP-A-NOSE

MY mother and your mother
Went over the way;
Said my mother to your mother,
It's chop-a-nose day.

The child's nose is held between finger and thumb and chopped off smartly with the other hand.

PEOPLE

MOTHER SHUTTLE

OLD Mother Shuttle
Lived in a coal-scuttle
Along with her dog and her cat;
  What they ate I can't tell,
  But 'tis known very well
That not one of the party was fat.

  Old Mother Shuttle
  Scoured out her coal-scuttle,
And washed both her dog and her
    cat;
  The cat scratched her nose,
  So they came to hard blows,
And who was the gainer by that?

TAILOR OF BICESTER

THE tailor of Bicester,
  He has but one eye;
He cannot cut a pair of green
    galligaskins,
  If he were to die.

CHARLES I

As I was going by Charing Cross,
I saw a black man upon a black
  horse;
They told me it was King Charles
  the First—
Oh dear, my heart was ready to
  burst!

MAN IN THE MOON

THE Man in the Moon was caught
  in a trap
For stealing the thorns from another
  man's gap.
If he had gone by, and let the thorns
  lie,
He'd never been Man in the Moon
  so high.

PETER

PETER, Peter, pumpkin eater,
Had a wife and couldn't keep her;
He put her in a pumpkin shell
And there he kept her **very** well.

Peter, Peter, pumpkin eater,
Had another, and didn't love her;
Peter learned to read and spell,
And then he loved her very well.

THE MAN IN THE MOON

THE man in the moon
Came down too soon,
And asked his way to Norwich;
He went by the south,
And burnt his mouth
With supping cold plum porridge.

LACK WIT

WHEN I was a little boy
I had but little wit;
'Tis a long time ago,
And I have no more yet;
Nor ever, ever shall,
Until that I die,
For the longer I live
The more fool am I.

THE WISE MEN OF GOTHAM

THREE wise men of Gotham
Went to sea in a bowl;
If the bowl had been stronger,
My story would have been longer.

ROBINSON CRUSOE

POOR old Robinson Crusoe!
Poor old Robinson Crusoe!
He made him a coat,
Of an old nanny goat,
   What a clever fellow to do so!
With a ring a ting tang,
And a ring a ting tang,
   Poor old Robinson Crusoe!

JERRY HALL

JERRY Hall,
He is so small,
A rat could eat him,
Hat and all.

THE MAN IN THE MOON

THE man in the moon drinks claret,
But he is a dull jack-a-dandy;
Would he know a sheep's head from
    a carrot,
He should learn to drink cider and
    brandy.

JOLLY MILLER

THERE was a jolly miller once,
    Lived on the river Dee;
He worked and sang from morn till
        night,
    No lark more blithe than he.
And this the burden of his song
    Forever used to be,
I care for nobody, no! not I,
    If nobody cares for me.

THE GIANT

FEE, fi, fo, fum,
I smell the blood of an Englishman:
Be he alive or be he dead,
I'll grind his bones to make my bread.

JOHN JIGGY JAG

LITTLE John Jiggy Jag,
He rode a penny nag,
    And went to Wigan to woo:
When he came to a beck,
He fell and broke his neck,
    Johnny, how dost thou now?

I made him a hat
Of my coat lap,
    And stockings of pearly blue;
A hat and a feather,
To keep out cold weather,
    So, Johnny, how dost thou now?

NANCY COCK

UP hill and down dale,
Butter is made in every vale,
And if that Nancy Cock
Is a good girl,
She shall have a spouse
And make butter anon,
Before her old grandmother
Grows a young man.

SULKY SUE

HERE's Sulky Sue;
What shall we do?
Turn her face to the wall
Till she comes to.

ROBIN THE BOBBIN

ROBIN the Bobbin,
 the big-bellied Ben,
He ate more meat
 than fourscore men;
He ate a cow,
 he ate a calf,
He ate a butcher
 and a half,
He ate a church,
 he ate a steeple,
He ate a priest
 and all the people!
A cow and a calf,
An ox and a half,
A church and a steeple,
And all the good people,
And yet he complained
 that his stomach wasn't full.

THE DAME OF DUNDEE

THERE was an old woman
 Who lived in Dundee,
And in her back garden
 There grew a plum tree;
The plums they grew rotten
 Before they grew ripe,
And she sold them
 Three farthings a pint.

CHARLEY WARLIE

CHARLEY Warlie had a cow,
Black and white about the brow;
Open the gate and let her through,
Charley Warlie's old cow.

84

CROSS-PATCH

CROSS-PATCH,
Draw the latch,
Sit by the fire and spin;
Take a cup,
And drink it up,
Then call your neighbours in.

THE DEVIL

ST. DUNSTAN, as the story goes,
Once pulled the devil by his nose,
With red hot tongs, which made
    him roar,
That could be heard ten miles or
    more.

ROBIN AND RICHARD

ROBIN and Richard
  Were two pretty men,
They lay in bed
  Till the clock struck ten;
Then up starts Robin
  And looks at the sky,
Oh, brother Richard,
  The sun's very high.
You go before
  With the bottle and bag,
And I will come after
  On little Jack Nag.

KING PIPPIN

LITTLE King Pippin
  He built a fine hall,
Pie-crust and pastry-crust
  That was the wall;
The windows were made
  Of black pudding and white,
And slated with pancakes,
  You ne'er saw the like.

ONE-EYED GUNNER

THERE was a little one-eyed gunner,
Who killed all the birds that died
last summer.

HARRY PARRY

OH, rare Harry Parry,
  When will you marry?
When apples and pears are ripe.
I'll come to your wedding
Without any bidding,
And dance and sing all the night.

CHARLEY BARLEY

CHARLEY Barley, butter and eggs,
Sold his wife for three duck eggs.
When the ducks began to lay
Charley Barley flew away.

TOM BROWN'S INDIANS

TOM Brown's two little Indian boys;
  One ran away,
  The other wouldn't stay,
Tom Brown's two little Indian boys.

TEN O'CLOCK SCHOLAR

A DILLER, a dollar,
A ten o'clock scholar,
What makes you come so soon?
You used to come at ten o'clock,
But now you come at noon.

BETTY BLUE

LITTLE Betty Blue
  Lost her holiday shoe,
What can little Betty do?
  Give her another
  To match the other,
And then she may walk out in two.

OLD BONIFACE

OLD Boniface he loved good cheer,
  And took his glass of Burton,
And when the nights grew sultry hot
  He slept without a shirt on.

OLD PUDDING-PIE WOMAN

THERE was an old woman
  Sold puddings and pies;
She went to the mill
  And dust blew in her eyes.
Hot puddings, and cold puddings,
  And nice pies to sell;
Wherever she goes, if you have a
    good nose,
  You may follow her by the smell.

LITTLE HUSBAND

I HAD a little husband,
  No bigger than my thumb;
I put him in a pint pot
  And there I bade him drum.
I gave him some garters
  To garter up his hose,
And a little silk handkerchief
  To wipe his pretty nose.

A TAWNYMOOR

As I went by a dyer's door,
I met a lusty tawnymoor;
Tawny hands, and tawny face,
Tawny petticoats,
Silver lace.

Old Mother Goose,
　When she wanted to wander,
Would ride through the air
　On a very fine gander.

Mother Goose had a house,
　'Twas built in a wood,
Where an owl at the door
　For sentinel stood.

She had a son Jack,
　A plain-looking lad,
He was not very good,
　Nor yet very bad.

She sent him to market,
　A live goose he bought;
See, mother, says he,
　I have not been for nought.

Jack's goose and her gander
　Grew very fond;
They'd both eat together,
　Or swim in the pond.

Jack found one fine morning,
　As I have been told,
His goose had laid him
　An egg of pure gold.

and the Golden Egg ┄┄┄┄

Jack ran to his mother
  The news for to tell,
She called him a good boy,
  And said it was well.

Jack sold his gold egg
  To a merchant untrue,
Who cheated him out of
  A half of his due.

Then Jack went a-courting
  A lady so gay,
As fair as the lily,
  And sweet as the May.

The merchant and squire
  Soon came at his back,
And began to belabour
  The sides of poor Jack.

Then old Mother Goose
  That instant came in,
And turned her son Jack
  Into famed Harlequin.

She then with her wand
  Touched the lady so fine,
And turned her at once
  Into sweet Columbine.

The gold egg in the sea
　　Was thrown away then,
When an odd fish brought her
　　The egg back again.

The merchant then vowed
　　The goose he would kill,
Resolving at once
　　His pockets to fill.

Jack's mother came in,
　　And caught the goose soon,
And mounting its back,
　　Flew up to the moon.

THE BACHELOR'S LAMENT

WHEN I was a little boy
　　I lived by myself,
And all the bread and cheese I got
　　I laid upon a shelf.

The rats and the mice
　　They made such a strife,
I had to go to London town
　　And get me a wife.

The wheelbarrow broke
　　And my wife had a fall,
Farewell wheelbarrow,
　　Little wife and all.

The streets were so broad
　　And the lanes were so narrow,
I was forced to bring my wife home
　　In a wheelbarrow.

Taffies

Taffy was a Welshman,
  Taffy was a thief,
Taffy came to my house
  And stole a piece of beef.

I went to Taffy's house,
  Taffy wasn't in,
I jumped upon his Sunday hat
  And poked it with a pin.

Taffy was a Welshman,
  Taffy was a cheat,
Taffy came to my house
  And stole a piece of meat.

Taffy was a Welshman,
  Taffy was a sham,
Taffy came to my house
  And stole a leg of lamb.

I went to Taffy's house,
  Taffy was not there,
I hung his coat and trousers
  To roast before a fire.

I went to Taffy's house,
  Taffy wasn't home;
Taffy came to my house
  And stole a marrow bone.

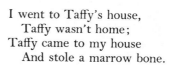

Taffy was born
  On a moonshiny night,
His head in a pipkin,
  His heels upright.

Little Johnny Morgan,
  Gentleman of Wales,
Came riding on a nanny-goat,
  Selling of pigs' tails.

Feasts

Mr. East gave a feast;
Mr. North laid the cloth;
Mr. West did his best;
Mr. South burnt his mouth
With eating a cold potato.

GREEDY TOM

Jimmy the Mowdy
Made a great crowdy;
Barney O'Neal
Found all the meal;
Old Jack Rutter
Sent two stone of butter;
The Laird of the Hot
Boiled it in his pot;
And Big Tom of the Hall
He supped it all.

THREE GHOSTESSES

Three little ghostesses,
Sitting on postesses,
Eating buttered toastesses,
Greasing their fistesses,
Up to their wristesses.
Oh, what beastesses
To make such feastesses!

SANDY KILDANDY

Sandy Kildandy,
The Laird o' Kilnap,
Suppit his brose
And swallowed his caup.
And after a'
He wasna fu';
He gaed tae the byre
And swallowed the coo.

HANNAH BANTRY

Hannah Bantry,
In the pantry,
Gnawing at a mutton bone;
How she gnawed it,
How she clawed it,
When she found herself alone.

CHARLIE WAG

Charlie Wag,
Charlie Wag,
Ate the pudding
And left the bag.

Furores

MRS. MASON'S BASIN

MRS. MASON bought a basin,
Mrs. Tyson said, What a nice 'un,
What did it cost? said Mrs. Frost,
Half a crown, said Mrs. Brown,
Did it indeed, said Mrs. Reed,
It did for certain, said Mrs. Burton.
Then Mrs. Nix up to her tricks
Threw the basin on the bricks.

FIRE! FIRE!

FIRE! Fire! said the town crier;
Where? Where? said Goody
  Blair;
Down the town, said Goody
  Brown;
I'll go and see't, said Goody
  Fleet;
So will I, said Goody Fry.

PEG

THERE was an old woman, her
  name was Peg;
Her head was of wood and she
  wore a cork leg.
The neighbours all pitched her
  into the water,
Her leg was drowned first, and
  her head followed after.

NOTHING-AT-ALL

THERE was an old woman called Nothing-
  at-all,
Who lived in a dwelling exceedingly
  small;
A man stretched his mouth to its utmost
  extent,
And down at one gulp house and old
  woman went.

THE GOSSIPS

MISS One, Two, and Three
  Could never agree,
While they gossiped around
  A tea-caddy.

DECEIVER

THERE was an old man in a velvet coat,
He kissed a maid and gave her a groat;
The groat was cracked and would not go,
Ah, old man, do you serve me so?

Who comes here?
  A grenadier.
What do you want?
  A pot of beer.
Where's your money?
  I forgot it.
Get you gone,
  You silly blockhead.

Or: Where's your money? I have
  none.
Then Grenadier, get you gone.

MOTHER NIDDITY NOD

Old Mother Niddity Nod
Swore by the pudding-bag,
She would go to Stoken Church fair;
Then old Father Peter
Said he would meet her,
Before she got half-way there.

MY LITTLE WIFE

I had a little wife,
  The prettiest ever seen;
She washed up the dishes,
  And kept the house clean.
She went to the mill
  To fetch me some flour,
And always got home
  In less than an hour.
She baked me my bread,
  She brewed me my ale,
She sat by the fire
  And told many a fine tale.

AN OLD WOMAN

There was an old woman
  Lived under a hill,
She put a mouse in a bag,
  And sent it to the mill.
The miller did swear
  By the point of his knife,
He never took toll
  Of a mouse in his life.

94

FOUR CHILDREN

WILLIAM and Mary,
  George and Anne,
Four such children
  Had never a man:
They put their father
  To flight and shame,
And called their brother
  A shocking bad name.

JOHN WATTS

PRETTY John Watts,
  We are troubled with rats,
Will you drive them out of the
  house?
    We have mice, too, in plenty,
    That feast in the pantry;
    But let them stay,
    And nibble away:
What harm is a little brown mouse?

SNAIL HUNTERS

FOUR and twenty tailors
  Went to kill a snail,
The best man amongst them
  Durst not touch her tail;
She put out her horns
  Like a little Kyloe cow,
Run, tailors, run,
  Or she'll kill you all e'en now.

JACK AND GYE

JACK and Gye
  Went out in the rye,
And they found a little boy
  With one black eye.
Come, says Jack,
  Let's knock him on the head.
No, says Gye,
  Let's buy him some bread;
You buy one loaf
  And I'll buy two,
And we'll bring him up
  As other folks do.

JACK A NORY

I'LL tell you a story
  About Jack a Nory,
And now my story's begun;
  I'll tell you another
  Of Jack and his brother,
And now my story is done.

DINGTY diddlety,
　　My mammy's maid,
She stole oranges,
　　I am afraid;
Some in her pocket,
　　Some in her sleeve,
She stole oranges,
　　I do believe.

MASTER AND MAN

MASTER I have, and I am his man,
　　Galloping dreary dun,
Master I have, and I am his man,
And he'll get a wife as fast as he can,
　　With a haily gaily, gambo raily,
　　Gigg'ling, nigg'ling, galloping galloway,
　　Draggle tail, dreary dun.

LITTLE MOPPET

I HAD a little moppet,
I kept it in my pocket
And fed it on corn and hay;
There came a proud beggar
And said he would wed her,
And stole my little moppet
　　away.

ABRAM BROWN

OLD Abram Brown is dead and gone,
　　You'll never see him more;
He used to wear a long brown coat
　　That buttoned down before.

THE HEN KEEPER

THERE was an old man who lived in
　　Middle Row,
He had five hens and a name for
　　them, oh!
Bill and Ned and Battock,
Cut-her-foot and Pattock;
Chuck, my lady Pattock,
Go to thy nest and lay.

WILLIAM McTRIMBLETOE

WILLIAM McTrimbletoe,
He's a good fisherman,
Catches fishes,
Puts them in dishes,
Catches hens,
Puts them in pens;
Some lay eggs,
Some lay none,
William McTrimbletoe
He doesn't eat one.

LITTLE BLUE BETTY

LITTLE Blue Betty lived in a den,
She sold good ale to gentlemen;
Gentlemen came every day,
And little Blue Betty hopped away,
She hopped upstairs to make her bed,
And she tumbled down and broke her head.

THE SCAREDY

THERE was a little boy went into
    a barn,
    And lay down on some hay;
An owl came out and flew about,
    And the little boy ran away.

SILLY

GILLY Silly Jarter,
She lost her garter,
    In a shower of rain.
The miller found it,
    The miller ground it,
And the miller gave it to Silly again.

BETSY BAKER

GOOSEY, goosey gander,
Who stands yonder?
Little Betsy Baker;
Take her up and shake her.

TERENCE McDIDDLER

TERENCE McDiddler,
    The three-stringed fiddler,
Can charm, if you please,
    The fish from the seas.

PUNCH and Judy
   Fought for a pie;
Punch gave Judy
   A knock in the eye.
Says Punch to Judy,
   Will you have any more?
Says Judy to Punch,
   My eye is too sore.

DOCTOR FELL

I DO not like thee, Doctor Fell,
The reason why I cannot tell;
But this I know, and know full well,
I do not like thee, Doctor Fell.

A LITTLE MAID

THERE was a little maid, and she
   was afraid
That her sweetheart would come
   unto her;
So she went to bed, and covered up
   her head,
And fastened the door with a skewer.

OLD BANDY LEGS

As I was going to sell my eggs,
I met a man with bandy legs;
Bandy legs and crooked toes,
I tripped up his heels and he fell on
   his nose.

DOCTOR FOSTER

DOCTOR Foster went to Gloucester
In a shower of rain;
He stepped in a puddle,
Right up to his middle,
And never went there again.

TOMMY TROT

TOMMY Trot, a man of law,
Sold his bed and lay upon straw;
Sold the straw and slept on grass,
To buy his wife a looking-glass.

THE BAD RIDER

I HAD a little pony,
  His name was Dapple Gray;
I lent him to a lady
  To ride a mile away.
She whipped him, she slashed him,
  She rode him through the mire;
I would not lend my pony now,
  For all the lady's hire.

TOMMY TACKET

LITTLE Tommy Tacket
Sits upon his cracket;
Half a yard of cloth
Will make him coat and jacket;
Make him coat and jacket,
Breeches to the knee,
And if you will not have him,
You may let him be.

HECTOR PROTECTOR

HECTOR Protector was dressed all in
  green;
Hector Protector was sent to the
  Queen.
The Queen did not like him,
No more did the King;
So Hector Protector was sent back
  again.

LITTLE GIRL

LITTLE girl, little girl,
  Where have you been?
I've been to see grandmother
  Over the green.
What did she give you?
  Milk in a can.
What did you say for it?
  Thank you, Grandam.

THE DUNCE

RING the bells, ring!
Hip, hurrah for the King!
The dunce fell into the pool, oh!
The dunce was going to school, oh!
The groom and the cook
Fished him out with a hook,
And he piped his eye like a fool, oh!

WHEN I was a little girl,
  About seven years old,
I hadn't got a petticoat,
  To keep me from the cold.

So I went into Darlington,
  That pretty little town,
And there I bought a petticoat,
  A cloak, and a gown.

ROBIN-A-BOBBIN

ROBIN-A-BOBBIN
He bent his bow,
Shot at a pigeon
And killed a crow;
Shot at another
And killed his own brother,
Did Robin-a-bobbin
Who bent his bow.

I went into the woods
  And built me a kirk,
And all the birds of the air,
  They helped me to work.

The hawk, with his long claws,
  Pulled down the stone;
The dove with her rough bill,
  Brought me them home.

The parrot was the clergyman,
  The peacock was the clerk,
The bullfinch played the organ,
  And we made merry work.

DAME TROT

DAME Trot and her cat
  Sat down for a chat;
The Dame sat on this side
  And puss sat on that.

Puss, says the Dame,
  Can you catch a rat,
Or a mouse in the dark?
  Purr, says the cat.

100

DOB AND MOB

THERE was a man,
  And his name was Dob,
And he had a wife,
  And her name was Mob.
And he had a dog,
  And he called it Bob,
And she had a cat,
  Called Chitterabob.
    Bob, says Dob;
    Chitterabob, says Mob.
Bob was Dob's dog,
  Chitterabob Mob's cat.

GREGORY GRIGGS

GREGORY Griggs, Gregory Griggs,
Had twenty-seven different wigs.
He wore them up, he wore them
  down,
To please the people of the town;
He wore them east, he wore them
  west,
But he never could tell which he
  loved the best.

LITTLE BLUE BEN

LITTLE Blue Ben, who lives in the
  glen,
Keeps a blue cat and one blue hen,
Which lays of blue eggs a score and
  ten;
Where shall I find the little Blue
  Ben?

ELSIE MARLEY

ELSIE Marley is grown so fine,
She won't get up to feed the swine,
But lies in bed till eight or nine.
    Lazy Elsie Marley.

MR. IBISTER

MR. IBISTER, and Betsy his sister,
Resolved upon giving a treat;
    So letters they write,
    Their friends to invite,
To their house in Great Camomile
    Street.

DOCTOR FOSTER

DOCTOR Foster is a good man,
He teaches children all he can:
Reading, writing, arithmetic,
And doesn't forget to use his stick.
When he does he makes them dance
Out of England into France,
Out of France into Spain,
Round the world and back again.

101

MAN OF DERBY

A LITTLE old man of Derby,
How do you think he served me?
He took away my bread and cheese,
And that is how he served me.

DICKY DILVER

LITTLE Dicky Dilver
Had a wife of silver;
He took a stick and broke her back
And sold her to the miller;
The miller wouldn't have her
So he threw her in the river.

THREE COOKS

THERE were three cooks of Cole-
brook,
And they fell out with our cook;
And all was for a pudding he took
From the three cooks of Colebrook.

JOHNNY ARMSTRONG

JOHNNY Armstrong killed a calf,
Peter Henderson got half,
Willy Wilkinson got the head,
Ring the bell, the calf is dead.

JOHNNIE NORRIE

JOHNNIE Norrie
Gaed up three paper stairies
And in at a paper doorie.

A LITTLE
LEARNING

A B C D
E F G
H I J K
L-M-N-O-P
Q R S T
U and V
W X Y Z-z-Z !

And here's the child's Dad,
Who is sagacious and discerning,
And knows this is the fount of
    learning.

A, B, C, D, E, F, G,
Little Robin Redbreast sitting on a tree;
H, I, J, K, L, M, N,
He made love to little Jenny Wren;
O, P, Q, R, S, T, U,
Dear little Jenny, I want to marry you.
V, W, X, Y, Z,
Poor little Jenny she blushed quite red.

AND BACKWARDS

Z, Y, X, and W, V,
U, T, S, and R, Q, P,
O, N, M, and L, K, J,
I, H, G,
F, E, D,
And C, B, A.

GREAT A was alarmed at B's bad behaviour,
Because C, D, E, F. denied G a favour,
H had a husband with I, J, K, and L,
M married Mary and taught her scholars how to spell;
A, B, C, D, E, F, G, H, I, J, K, L, M, N,
O, P, Q, R, S, T, U, V, W, X, Y, Z.

THE GOOD BOY

A BOY that is good
    Will learn his book well;
And if he can't read
    Will strive for to spell.

105

TOM THUMB'S

A was an archer,
       who shot at a frog;
B was a butcher,
       and had a great dog.
C was a captain,
       all covered with lace;
D was a drunkard,
       and had a red face.
E was an esquire,
       with pride on his brow;
F was a farmer,
       and followed the plough.
G was a gamester,
       who had but ill-luck;
H was a hunter,
       and hunted a buck.
I was an innkeeper,
       who loved to carouse;
J was a joiner,
       and built up a house.
K was King William,
       once governed this land;
L was a lady,
       who had a white hand.
M was a miser,
       and hoarded up gold;

106

PICTURE ALPHABET

N was a nobleman,
   gallant and bold.
O was an oyster girl,
   and went about town;
P was a parson,
   and wore a black gown.
Q was a queen,
   who wore a silk slip;
R was a robber,
   and wanted a whip.
S was a sailor,
   and spent all he got;
T was a tinker,
   and mended a pot.
U was a userer,
   a miserable elf;
V was a vintner,
   who drank all himself.
W was a watchman,
   and guarded the door;
X was expensive,
   and so became poor.
Y was a youth,
   that did not love school;
Z was a zany,
   a poor harmless fool.

The Tragical Death of A, Apple Pie

A B C D E F G H I J K L M N O P Q R S T U V W X Y Z

WHO WAS CUT IN PIECES,

AND EATEN BY TWENTY-SIX GENTLEMEN,

WITH WHOM ALL LITTLE PEOPLE

Ought to be Very Well Acquainted

A was an
Apple pie

B
Bit it

C
Cut it

D
Dealt it

E
Eat it

F
Fought for it

G
Got it

H
Had it

I
Inspected it

J
Joined for it

K
Kept it

L
Longed for it

M
Mourned for it

N
Nodded at it

O
Opened it

P
Peeped in it

Q
Quartered it

R
Ran for it

S
Stole it

T
Took it

U
Upset it

V
Viewed it

W
Wanted it

XYZ and **&**
All wished for
a piece in hand

109

Counting Cherry Stones

Tinker,   Soldier,   Rich man,   Beggar man,
    Tailor,   Sailor,   Poor man,   Thief.

SOLDIER brave, Sailor true,
Skilled physician, Oxford Blue,
Learned lawyer, Squire so hale,
Dashing airman, Curate pale.

ARMY, Navy,
Medicine, Law,
Church, Nobility,
Nothing at all.

A LAIRD, a lord,
   A cooper, a thief,
A piper, a drummer,
   A stealer of beef.

LADY,
Baby,
Gipsy,
Queen.

ARMY, Navy,
Peerage, Trade,
Doctor, Divinity,
Law.

THE WEDDING

THIS year,
Next year,
Sometime,
Never.

COACH,
Carriage,
Wheelbarrow,
Dust cart.

GOLD,
Silver,
Copper,
Brass.

SILK,
Satin,
Cotton,
Rags.

BIG box,
Little box,
Band box,
Bundle.

BOOTS,
Shoes,
Slippers,
Clogs.

CHURCH,
Chapel,
Cathedral,
Abbey.

BIG house,
Little house,
Pig sty,
Barn.

Chinese Counting

One-ery, two-ery, tickery, seven,
Hallibo, crackibo, ten and eleven,
Spin, span, muskidan,
Twiddle-um, twaddle-um, twenty-
    one.

Intery, mintery, cutery, corn,
Apple seed and briar thorn;
Wire, briar, limber lock,
Five geese in a flock,
Sit and sing by a spring,
O-U-T, and in again.

Inter, mitzy, titzy, tool,
Ira, dira, dominu,
Oker, poker, dominoker,
Out goes you.

Eena, meena, mina, mo,
Catch a tigger by his toe;
If he squeals, let him go,
Eena, meena, mina, mo.

Eeny, weeny, winey, wo,
Where do all the Frenchmen go?
To the east and to the west
And into the old crow's nest.

Eenie, meenie, mackeracka,
Hi, di, dominacka,
Stickeracka, roomeracka,
Om, pom, push.

One-ery, two-ery, ickery, Ann,
Phillisy, phollisy, Nicholas John,
Quever, quaver, Irish Mary,
Stickerum, stackerum, buck.

One-erum, two-erum,
Cockerum, shu-erum,
Shetherum, shatherum,
Wineberry, wagtail,
Tarrydiddle, den.

Hickety, pickety, i-silicity,
Pompalorum jig,
Every man who has no hair
Generally wears a wig.

Ah, ra, chickera,
Roly, poly, pickena,
Kinny, minny, festi,
Shanti-poo,
Ickerman, chickerman, chinee-choo.

Ala, mala, mink, monk,
Tink, tonk, toozey,
Oozy, voozy, aggardy,
Ah, vah, vack.

Eenity, feenity, fickety, feg,
El, del, domen, egg,
Irky, birky, story, rock,
An, tan, toosh, Jock.

111

Numbers

1, 2,
Buckle my shoe;

3, 4,
Knock at the door;

5, 6,
Pick up sticks;

7, 8,
Lay them straight;

9, 10,
A big fat hen;

11, 12,
Dig and delve;

13, 14,
Maids a-courting;

15, 16,
Maids in the kitchen;

17, 18,
Maids in waiting;

19, 20,
My plate's empty.

ROMAN FIGURES

X shall stand for playmates Ten;
V for Five stout stalwart men;
I for One, as I'm alive;
C for Hundred, and D for Five;
M for a Thousand soldiers true,
And L for Fifty, I'll tell you.

ONE, TWO, THREE, FOUR

ONE, two, three, four,
Mary at the cottage door,
Five, six, seven, eight,
Eating cherries off a plate.

ONE, TWO, THREE, FOUR, FIVE

ONE, two, three, four, five,
Once I caught a fish alive,
Six, seven, eight, nine, ten,
Then I let it go again.
Why did you let it go?
Because it bit my finger so.
Which finger did it bite?
The little finger on the right.

DAYS IN THE MONTH

THIRTY days hath September,
April, June, and November;
All the rest have thirty-one,
Excepting February alone,
And that has twenty-eight days clear
And twenty-nine in each leap year.

LITTLE HUNDRED

ONE's none,
Two's some,
Three's many,
Four's a penny,
Five's a little hundred.

Kings and Queens

'NO PLAN LIKE YOURS TO STUDY HISTORY WISELY'
(Norman, Plantagenet, Lancaster, York, Tudor,
Stuart, Hanover, Windsor)

First William the Norman,
    Then William his son;
Henry, Stephen, and Henry,
    Then Richard and John;
Next Henry the third,
    Edwards, one, two, and three,
And again after Richard
    Three Henrys we see.
Two Edwards, third Richard,
    If rightly I guess;
Two Henrys, sixth Edward,
    Queen Mary, Queen Bess.
Then Jamie the Scotchman,
    Then Charles whom they slew,
Yet received after Cromwell
    Another Charles too.

Next James the second
    Ascended the throne;
Then good William and Mary
    Together came on.
Till Anne, Georges four,
    And fourth William all past,
Came the reign of Victoria,
    Which longest did last.
Then Edward the Peacemaker,
    He was her son,
And the fifth of the Georges
    Was next in the run;
Edward the Eighth
    Gave the crown to his brother,
Now God's sent Elizabeth:
    All of us love her.

FOUR DATES

William the Conqueror, ten sixty-six,
Played on the Saxons oft-cruel tricks.

Columbus sailed the ocean blue,
In fourteen hundred and ninety-two.

The Spanish Armada met its fate,
In fifteen hundred and eighty-eight.

In sixteen hundred and sixty-six,
London burnt like rotten sticks.

113

Good Counsel

THE cock doth crow
To let you know
If you be wise
'Tis time to rise:
For early to bed,
And early to rise,
Is the way to be healthy
And wealthy and wise.

Go to bed late,
Stay very small;
Go to bed early,
Grow very tall.

PATIENCE is a virtue,
    Virtue is a grace;
Both put together
    Make a very pretty face.

ONE thing at a time
    And that done well,
Is a very good rule,
    As many can tell.

To sleep easy all night,
Let your supper be light,
Or else you'll complain
Of a stomach in pain.

BUTTON to chin
When October comes in;
Cast not a clout
Till May be out.

HE that would thrive
Must rise at five;
He that hath thriven
May lie till seven;
He that will never thrive
May lie till eleven.

SAY well and do well
    End with one letter;
Say well is good,
    Do well is better.

GOOD, better, best;
Never rest
Till 'good' be 'better',
And 'better' 'best'.

ONE, two, whatever you do,
Start it well and carry it through.
Try, try, never say die,
Things will come right,
    you know, by and by.

REWARD

WHEN Jacky's a good boy,
    He shall have cakes and custard;
But when he does nothing but cry,
    He shall have nothing but mustard.

114

Good Manners

MANNERS in the dining-room,
    Manners in the hall,
If you don't behave yourself
    You shan't have none at all.

OF a little take a little,
    You're kindly welcome, too;
Of a little leave a little,
    'Tis manners so to do.

COME when you're called,
    Do as you're bid,
Shut the door after you,
    Never be chid.

SPEAK when you're spoken to,
    Come for one call,
Shut the door after you,
    Turn to the wall.

HOLD up your head,
    Turn out your toes,
Speak when you're spoken to,
    Mend your clothes.

WILFUL waste brings woeful want
    And you may live to say,
How I wish I had that crust
    That once I threw away.

PUNCTUALITY

FIRST in a carriage,
    Second in a gig,
Third on a donkey,
    And fourth on a pig.

HEARTS, like doors, will ope with
    ease
    To very, very, little keys,
And don't forget that two of these
    Are 'I thank you' and 'If you
      please'.

BE always in time,
Too late is a crime.

GRACE

GOD bless our meat,
God guide our ways,
God give us grace
Our Lord to please.
Lord, long preserve in peace and health
Our gracious Queen Elizabeth.

This grace was repeated in the time of the first Queen Elizabeth.

Worldly Wise

Of all the sayings in this world
  The one to see you through
Is, Never trouble trouble
  Till trouble troubles you.

If wishes were horses
  Beggars would ride;
If turnips were watches
  I would wear one by my side.

For want of a nail
  The shoe was lost,
For want of a shoe
  The horse was lost,
For want of a horse
  The rider was lost,
For want of a rider
  The battle was lost,
For want of a battle
  The kingdom was lost,
And all for the want
  Of a horse shoe nail.

Penny and penny
Laid up will be many;
Who will not save a penny
Shall never have many.

For every evil under the sun,
There is a remedy or there is none.
If there be one, try and find it;
If there be none, never mind it.

Scissors and string, scissors and
    string,
When a man's single he lives like a
    king.
Needles and pins, needles and pins,
When a man marries his trouble
    begins.

A wise old owl sat in an oak,
The more he heard the less he spoke;
The less he spoke the more he heard.
Why aren't we all like that wise old
    bird?

To make your candles last for aye,
  You wives and maids give ear-o;
To put 'em out's the only way,
  Says honest John Boldero.

When land is gone and money spent,
Then learning is most excellent.

Weather
Wise

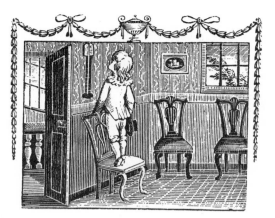

EVENING red and morning grey,
Send the traveller on his way;
Evening grey and morning red,
Bring the rain upon his head.

WHEN the wind is in the east,
'Tis neither good for man nor beast;
When the wind is in the north,
The skilful fisher goes not forth;
When the wind is in the south,
It blows the bait in the fishes' mouth;
When the wind is in the west,
Then 'tis at the very best.

WHEN the clouds are upon the hills,
They'll come down by the mills.

WHEN the dew is on the grass,
Rain will never come to pass.

IF the oak is out before the ash,
Then we'll only have a splash;
If the ash is out before the oak,
Then we'll surely have a soak.

RED sky at night,
Shepherd's delight;
Red sky in the morning,
Shepherd's warning.

RAIN before seven,
Fine before eleven.

A SUNSHINY shower
Won't last half an hour.

MACKEREL sky,
Mackerel sky,
Not long wet
And not long dry.

WHEN clouds appear
  Like rocks and towers,
The earth's refreshed
  By frequent showers.

IF bees stay at home,
Rain will soon come;
If they fly away,
Fine will be the day.

117

Observation

THE cuckoo comes in April,
He sings his song in May;
In the middle of June
He changes his tune,
And then he flies away.

A CHERRY year,
A merry year;
A pear year,
A dear year;
A plum year,
A dumb year.

ON the first of March
The crows begin to search;
By the first of April
They are sitting still;
By the first of May
They've all flown away,
Coming greedy back again
With October's wind and rain.

CUT thistles in May,
They grow in a day;
Cut them in June,
That is too soon;
Cut them in July,
Then they will die.

MARCH winds and April showers
Bring forth May flowers.

A SWARM of bees in May
Is worth a load of hay;
A swarm of bees in June
Is worth a silver spoon;
A swarm of bees in July
Is not worth a fly.

THROUGH storm and wind,
  Sunshine and shower,
Still will you find
  Groundsel in flower.

HAY is for horses,
  Straw is for cows,
Milk is for little pigs,
  And wash for old sows.

WHEN the wind blows,
Then the mill goes;
When the wind drops,
Then the mill stops.

ALL work and no play makes Jack a dull boy;
All play and no work makes Jack a mere toy.

AWAKENING

Towards Babylon

Little lad, little lad,
  Where were you born?
Far off in Lancashire,
  Under a thorn,
Where they sup butter-milk
  With a ram's horn;
And a pumpkin scoop'd
  With a yellow rim,
Is the bonny bowl
  They breakfast in.

I had a little nut tree,
  Nothing would it bear
But a silver nutmeg
  And a golden pear;
The king of Spain's daughter
  Came to visit me,
And all for the sake
  Of my little nut tree.
I skipped over water,
  I danced over sea,
And all the birds in the air
  Couldn't catch me.

Gray goose and gander,
  Waft your wings together,
And carry the good king's daughter
  Over the one-strand river.

As I went up the Brandy hill,
I met my father with good will;
He had jewels, he had rings,
He had many pretty things;
He'd a cat with nine tails,
He'd a hammer wanting nails.
Up Jock!
Down Tom!
Blow the bellows old man.

How many miles to Babylon?
Three-score and ten.
Can I get there by candle-light?
Yes, and back again.
If your heels are nimble and light,
You may get there by candle-light.

See-saw, sacradown,
Which is the way to London town?
One foot up and the other foot down,
That is the way to London town.

I went to the toad that lies under the wall,
I charmed him out, and he came at my call;
I scratched out the eyes of the owl before,
I tore the bat's wing: what would you have more?

Pretty Maids

THE rose is red, the rose is white,
The rose is in my garden;
I would not part with my sweetheart
For tuppence ha'penny farden.

ON Saturday night shall be my care
To powder my locks and curl my
hair;
On Sunday morning my love will
come in,
When he will marry me with a gold
ring.

BLOW the fire, blacksmith,
Make a lovely light.
Here comes a little girl
All dressed in white.
Fine shoes and stockings,
Fine curly hair,
Double ruff around her neck
And ne'er a smock to wear.

LITTLE pretty Nancy girl,
She sat upon the green,
Scouring of her candlesticks,
They were not very clean.
Her cupboard that was musty,
Her table that was dusty;
And pretty little Nancy girl,
She was not very lusty.

UP street and down street,
Each window's made of glass;
If you go to Tommy Tickler's
house
You'll find a pretty lass.

Hug her and kiss her,
And take her on your knee,
And whisper very close,
Darling girl, do you love me?

DOWN by the river
Where the green grass grows,
Pretty Polly Perkins
Bleaches her clothes.
She laughs and she sings,
And she sings so sweet.
She calls, Come over,
Across the street.
He kissed her, he kissed her,
He took her to the town;
He bought her a ring
And a damascene gown.

I HAD two pigeons bright and gay,
They flew from me the other day;
What was the reason they did go?
I cannot tell for I do not know.

and Pleasantries

As I was going up Pippen Hill,
  Pippen Hill was dirty.
There I met a pretty miss
  And she dropt me a curtsey.

Little miss, pretty miss,
  Blessings light upon you!
If I had half a crown a day,
  I'd spend it all upon you.

ONE misty, moisty morning,
  When cloudy was the weather,
There I met an old man
  Clothed all in leather.

Clothed all in leather,
  With cap under his chin:
How do you do, and how do you do,
  And how do you do again?

WHEN I was a little boy
  My mammy kept me in,
But now I am a great boy
  I'm fit to serve the king;
I can hand a musket,
  And I can smoke a pipe,
And I can kiss a bonny girl
  At twelve o'clock at night.

LITTLE Jack Dandy-prat
  Was my first suitor;
He had a dish and spoon
  And a little pewter;
He'd linen and woollen,
  And woollen and linen,
A little pig on a string
  Cost him five shilling.

MARGERY Mutton-pie
  And Johnny Bo-peep,
They met together
  In Gracechurch Street;
In and out, in and out,
  Over the way,
Oh, said Johnny,
  It's chop-a-nose day.

HEIGH ho! my heart is low,
  My mind is all on one;
It's W for I know who,
  And T for my love Tom.

OLD woman, old woman,
  Shall we go a-shearing?
Speak a little louder, sir,
  I'm very thick of hearing.
Old woman, old woman,
  Shall I love you dearly?
Thank you very kindly, sir,
  Now I hear you clearly.

Proposals

THERE was a little boy and a little
    girl,
  Lived in an alley;
Says the little boy to the little girl,
  Shall I, oh, shall I?

Says the little girl to the little boy,
  What shall we do?
Says the little boy to the little girl,
  I will kiss you.

CURLY locks, Curly locks,
  Wilt thou be mine?
Thou shalt not wash dishes
  Nor yet feed the swine;
But sit on a cushion
  And sew a fine seam,
And feed upon strawberries,
  Sugar and cream.

LITTLE maid, pretty maid,
  Whither goest thou?
Down in the forest
  To milk my cow.
Shall I go with thee?
  No, not now.
When I send for thee
  Then come thou.

SUKEY, you shall be my wife
  And I will tell you why:
I have got a little pig,
  And you have got a sty;
I have got a dun cow,
  And you can make good cheese;
Sukey, will you marry me?
  Say Yes, if you please.

A cow and a calf,
  An ox and a half,
Forty good shillings and three;
  Is that not enough tocher
  For a shoemaker's daughter,
A bonny lass with a black e'e?

I PEEPED through the window,
I peeped through the door,
I saw pretty Katie
A-dancing on the floor.
I cuddled her and fondled her,
I set her on my knee;
I says, Pretty Katie,
Won't you marry me?
A new-swept parlour,
A new-made bed,
A new cup and saucer
Against we get wed.

ONE I love,
Two I love,
Three I love, I say,
Four I love with all my heart,
Five I cast away;
Six he loves me,
Seven he don't,
Eight we're lovers both;
Nine he comes,
Ten he tarries,
Eleven he courts,
Twelve he marries.

O THE little rusty dusty miller,
Dusty was his coat,
Dusty was his colour,
Dusty was the kiss
I got from the miller.
If I had my pockets
Full of gold and siller,
I would give it all
To my dusty miller.

WILLY, Willy Wilkin,
Kissed the maids a-milking,
    Fa, la, la!
And with his merry daffing,
He set them all a-laughing,
    Ha, ha, ha!

HE loves me,
  He don't,
He'll have me,
  He won't,
He would
  If he could,
But he can't
  So he don't.

THIS is the key of the kingdom:
In that kingdom is a city,
In that city is a town,
In that town there is a street,
In that street there winds a lane,
In that lane there is a yard,
In that yard there is a house,
In that house there waits a room,
In that room there is a bed,
On that bed there is a basket,
  A basket of flowers.

Flowers in the basket,
Basket on the bed,
Bed in the chamber,
Chamber in the house,
House in the weedy yard,
Yard in the winding lane,
Lane in the broad street,
Street in the high town,
Town in the city,
City in the kingdom:
  This is the key of the kingdom.

Robin Hood, Robin Hood,
  Is in the mickle wood;
Little John, Little John,
  He to the town is gone.

Robin Hood, Robin Hood,
  Is telling his beads,
All in the green wood,
  Among the green weeds.

Little John, Little John,
  If he comes no more,
Robin Hood, Robin Hood,
  He will fret full sore.

As I was going up the hill,
  I met with Jack the piper;
And all the tune that he could play
  Was, 'Tie up your petticoats tighter'.

I tied them once, I tied them twice,
  I tied them three times over;
And all the song that he could sing
  Was, 'Carry me safe to Dover'.

I went to Noke
But nobody spoke;
I went to Thame,
It was just the same;
Burford and Brill
Were silent and still,
But I went to Beckley
And they spoke directly.

What is the rhyme for porringer?
What is the rhyme for porringer?
The king he had a daughter fair
And gave the Prince of Orange her.

At Brill on the hill
The wind blows shrill,
The cook no meat can dress;
At Stow-on-the-Wold
The wind blows cold,
I know no more than this.

Doodledy, doodledy, doodledy, dan,
I'll have a piper to be my good-man;
And if I get less meat, I shall have game,
Doodledy, doodledy, doodledy, dan.

It's once I courted as pretty a lass,
  As ever your eyes did see;
But now she's come to such a pass,
  She never will do for me.
She invited me to her house,
  Where oft I'd been before,
And she tumbled me into the hog-tub,
  And I'll never go there any more.

My mother said
That I never should
Play with the gipsies
In the wood;
If I did she would say,
Naughty girl to disobey.
Your hair shan't curl,
Your shoes shan't shine,
You naughty girl
You shan't be mine.
My father said
That if I did
He'd bang my head
With the teapot lid.

The wood was dark
The grass was green,
Up comes Sally
With a tambourine;
Alpaca frock,
New scarf-shawl,
White straw bonnet
And a pink parasol.
I went to the river—
No ship to get across,
I paid ten shillings
For an old blind horse;
I up on his back
And off in a crack,
Sally tell my mother
I shall never come back.

THE moon shines bright,
The stars give light,
And little Nanny Button-cap
Will come tomorrow night.

THE hart he loves the high wood,
    The hare she loves the hill;
The knight he loves his bright sword,
    The lady loves her will.

WINE and cakes for gentlemen,
    Hay and corn for horses,
A cup of ale for good old wives,
    And kisses for young lasses.

DAFFY-DOWN-DILLY is new come to town,
With a yellow petticoat, and a green gown.

JACKY, come give me thy fiddle,
    If ever you mean to thrive.
Nay, I'll not give my fiddle
    To any man alive.
If I should give my fiddle,
    They'll think that I'm gone mad,
For many a joyful day
    My fiddle and I have had.

I WON'T be my father's Jack,
I won't be my mother's Jill,
I will be the fiddler's wife
And have music when I will.
    T'other little tune,
    T'other little tune,
    Prithee, love, play me
    T'other little tune.

127

Songs in Season

NEW YEAR

GOD be here, God be there,
We wish you all a happy year;
God without, God within,
Let the Old Year out and the New
 Year in.

TWELFTH NIGHT

HERE's to thee, old apple tree,
Whence thou may'st bud
And whence thou may'st blow,
And whence thou may'st bear apples
 enow;
Hats full and caps full,
Bushels full and sacks full,
And our pockets full too.

ST. VALENTINE'S DAY

GOOD morrow to you, Valentine.
Curl your locks as I do mine,
Two before and three behind.
Good morrow to you, Valentine.

THE rose is red, the violet's blue,
The honey's sweet, and so are you.
Thou art my love and I am thine;
I drew thee to my Valentine.
The lot was cast and then I drew,
And fortune said it should be you.

MOTHERING SUNDAY

IT is the day of all the year,
Of all the year the one day,
And here come I, my Mother dear,
To bring you cheer,
A-mothering on Sunday.

SHROVETIDE

ONCE, twice, thrice,
I give thee warning,
Please to make pancakes
'Gin tomorrow morning.

GOOD FRIDAY

HOT cross buns, hot cross buns;
One a penny poker,
Two a penny tongs,
Three a penny fire shovel,
Hot cross buns.

EASTERTIDE

HERE's two or three jolly boys
 All of one mind,
We've come a pace-egging,
 And hope you'll be kind;
We hope you'll be kind
 With your eggs and your beer,
And we'll come no more pace-egging
 Until the next year.

MAY DAY

Good morning, Mistress and Master,
 I wish you a happy day;
Please to smell my garland
 'Cause it is the First of May.

A branch of May I have brought you,
 And at your door I stand;
It is but a sprout, but it's well
 budded out,
The work of our Lord's hand.

HARVEST

The boughs do shake and the bells
 do ring,
So merrily comes our harvest in,
Our harvest in, our harvest in,
So merrily comes our harvest in.

We've ploughed, we've sowed,
We've reaped, we've mowed,
We've got our harvest in.

GUNPOWDER PLOT DAY

Please to remember
The Fifth of November,
Gunpowder treason and plot;
I see no reason
Why gunpowder treason
Should ever be forgot.

CHRISTMAS-TIDE

St. Thomas's Day is past and gone,
And Christmas almost come,
 Maidens arise,
 And make your pies,
And save young Bobby some.

Christmas is coming,
 The geese are getting fat,
Please to put a penny
 In the old man's hat.
If you haven't got a penny,
 A ha'penny will do;
If you haven't got a ha'penny,
 Then God bless you!

Christmas comes but once a year,
And when it comes it brings good
 cheer,
A pocket full of money, and a cellar
 full of beer.

God bless the master of this house,
 And its good mistress too,
And all the little children
 That round the table go;
And all your kin and kinsmen,
 That dwell both far and near;
We wish you a merry Christmas
And a happy New Year.

129

Songs from Games

I WENT into my grandmother's
    garden
And there I found a farden;
I gave it to my mother
To buy a baby brother;
The baby was so bandy,
I gave it a drop of brandy;
The brandy was so hot,
I put it in the pot;
The pot was so little,
I put it in the kettle;
The kettle had a spout
And it all ran out.
    With a good push—
    Over the bowling green.

STOPPING THE SWING

Die, pussy, die,
Shut your little eye;
When you wake,
Find a cake—
Die, pussy, die.

BLIND MAN'S BUFF

BLIND man, blind man,
    Sure you can't see?
Turn round three times,
    And try to catch me.
Turn east, turn west,
    Catch as you can,
Did you think you'd caught me?
    Blind, blind man!

ALLIGOSHEE

DARBY and Joan were dressed in
    black,
Sword and buckle behind their back;
Foot for foot, and knee for knee,
Turn about Darby's company.

HERE COMES A WOOER

HERE comes a lusty wooer,
    My a dildin, my a daldin;
Here comes a lusty wooer,
    Lily bright and shine-a.

Pray, who do you woo,
    My a dildin, my a daldin?
Pray, who do you woo,
    Lily bright and shine-a?

I woo your fairest daughter,
    My a dildin, my a daldin;
I woo your fairest daughter,
    Lily bright and shine-a.

Then there she is for you,
    My a dildin, my a daldin;
Then there she is for you,
    Lily bright and shine-a.

TWIRLING

GREEN cheese, yellow laces,
Up and down the market places,
    Turn, cheeses, turn.

HERE'S A POOR WIDOW

HERE's a poor widow from Babylon,
With six poor children all alone;
One can bake, and one can brew,
One can shape, and one can sew,
One can sit at the fire and spin,
One can bake a cake for the king;
    Come choose you east,
    Come choose you west,
    Come choose the one
    You love the best.

GREEN GRASS

A DIS, a dis, a green grass,
  A dis, a dis, a dis;
Come all you pretty fair maids
  And dance along with us.

For we are going a-roving,
  A-roving in this land;
We'll take this pretty fair maid,
  We'll take her by the hand.

You shall have a duck, my dear,
  And you shall have a drake;
And you shall have a young prince,
  A young prince for your sake.

And if this young prince chance to
    die,
  You shall have another;
The bells will ring, and the birds will
    sing,
  And we'll all clap hands together.

CUCKOO, CHERRY TREE

CUCKOO, cuckoo, cherry tree,
Catch a bird, and give it me;
Let the tree be high or low,
Let it hail or rain or snow.

SALLY WATERS

SALLY, Sally Waters,
Sprinkle in the pan,
Rise Sally, rise Sally,
Choose a young man.
Bow to the east,
Bow to the west,
Bow to the young man
That you love best.

Now you are married
You must be good,
And help your wife
To chop the wood.
Chop it thin
And bring it in,
And kiss her over
  and over again.

THE BONNY CRAVAT

JENNY come tie my,
Jenny come tie my,
Jenny come tie my bonny cravat;
I've tied it behind,
I've tied it before,
I've tied it so often, I'll tie it
  no more.

DRAW A PAIL OF WATER

Draw a pail of water
For my lady's daughter;
My father's a king, and my mother's a queen,
My two little sisters are dressed in green,
Stamping grass and parsley,
  Marigold leaves and daisies.
One-a-me rush! Two-a-me rush!
Pray thee, young lady, creep under the bush.

Sieve my lady's oatmeal,
  Grind my lady's flour;
Put it in a chestnut,
  Let it stand an hour.
One-a-me rush! Two-a-me rush!
Pray thee, young lady, creep under the bush.

QUEEN ANNE

Lady Queen Anne she sits in the sun,
As fair as a lily, as white as a swan;
Come taste my lily, come smell my rose,
Which of my maidens do you choose?
The ball is ours and none of yours,
Go to the wood and gather flowers.
Cats and kittens now stay within,
While we young maidens walk out and in.

MY BANGALOREY MAN

Follow my Bangalorey Man;
Follow my Bangalorey Man;
I'll do all that ever I can
To follow my Bangalorey Man.
We'll borrow a horse, and steal a gig,
And round the world we'll do a jig,
  And I'll do all that ever I can
  To follow my Bangalorey Man.

WONDERS

If All the World was Paper

If all the world was paper,
  And all the sea was ink,
If all the trees were bread and cheese,
  What should we have to drink?

  It's enough to make a man like me
  Scratch his head and think.

TAMMY TYRIE

Wee Tammy Tyrie,
He jumped in the firie;
The fire wis ower hot,
He jumped in the pot;
The pot wis ower mettle,[1]
He jumped in the kettle;
The kettle wis ower wee,
He jumped in the sea;
The sea wis ower big,
He jumped on a pig;
The pig gae a roar,
He jumped on a boar;
The boar gae a bite,
And he ran to his Mammie,
Shouting, Mammie! Mammie!
  Mammie!

  [1] spirited, active

WHEN I WAS A LAD

When I was a lad and so was my dad
I came out of a bean swad;
The bean swad it was too full
And I jumped into a roaring bull;
The roaring bull it was too fat
And I jumped into a gentleman's hat;
The gentleman's hat it was too fine
So I jumped into a bottle of wine;
The bottle of wine it was too clear
So I jumped into a barrel of beer;
The barrel of beer it was too thick
So I jumped out on an oak stick;
The oak stick began to crack
And I jumped onto a horse's back;
The horse's back began to bend
So I jumped down by a turkey hen;
The turkey hen began to lay
And I got an egg that day for my tay.

I WOULD IF I COULD

I would, if I could,
If I couldn't how could I?
I couldn't, without I could,
    could I?
Could you, without you could,
    could ye?
Could ye? Could ye?
Could you, without you could,
    could ye?

OH THAT I WERE

Oh that I were
    Where I would be,
Then would I be
    Where I am not;
But where I am
    There I must be,
And where I would be
    I can not.

THERE was a man of double deed
Sowed his garden full of seed.
When the seed began to grow,
'Twas like a garden full of snow;
When the snow began to melt,
'Twas like a ship without a belt;
When the ship began to sail,
'Twas like a bird without a tail;
When the bird began to fly,
'Twas like an eagle in the sky;
When the sky began to roar,
'Twas like a lion at the door;
When the door began to crack,
'Twas like a stick across my back;
When my back began to smart,
'Twas like a penknife in my heart;
When my heart began to bleed,
'Twas death and death and death
    indeed.

THE sow came in with the saddle,
The little pig rocked the cradle,
The dish jumped up on the table
To see the pot swallow the ladle.
The spit that stood behind the door
Threw the pudding-stick on the floor.
  Odd's-bobs! says the gridiron,
    Can't you agree?
  I'm the head constable,
    Bring them to me.

THE rose is red, the grass is green,
Serve Queen Bess our noble queen.
  Kitty the spinner
  Will sit down to dinner,
And eat the leg of a frog:
  All you good people
  Look over the steeple,
And see the cat play with the dog.

I SAW a fishpond all on fire
I saw a house bow to a squire
I saw a parson twelve feet high
I saw a cottage near the sky
I saw a balloon made of lead
I saw a coffin drop down dead
I saw two sparrows run a race
I saw two horses making lace
I saw a girl just like a cat
I saw a kitten wear a hat
I saw a man who saw these too
And said though strange
    they all were true.

THERE was a king, and he had three
    daughters,
And they all lived in a basin of water;
  The basin bended,
  My story's ended.
If the basin had been stronger,
My story would have been longer.

If all the seas were one sea,
What a *great* sea that would be!
If all the trees were one tree,
What a *great* tree that would be!
And if all the axes were one axe,
What a *great* axe that would be!
And if all the men were one man,
What a *great* man that would be!
And if the *great* man took the *great* axe,
And cut down the *great* tree,
And let it fall into the *great* sea,
What a splish-splash that would be!

Upon Paul's steeple stands a tree
As full of apples as may be;
The little boys of London Town
They run with hooks to pull them down:
And then they run from hedge to hedge
Until they come to London Bridge.

There was an old woman
    And nothing she had,
And so this old woman
    Was said to be mad.
She'd nothing to eat,
    She'd nothing to wear,
She'd nothing to lose,
    She'd nothing to fear,
She'd nothing to ask,
    And nothing to give,
And when she did die
    She'd nothing to leave.

What's in there?
Gold and money.
Where's my share?
The mousie's run away
    with it.
Where's the mousie?
In her housie.
Where's her housie?
In the wood.
Where's the wood?
The fire burnt it.
Where's the fire?
The water quenched it.
Where's the water?
The brown bull drank it.
Where's the brown bull?
Behind Burnie's hill.
Where's Burnie's hill?
All dressed in snow.
Where's the snow?
The sun melted it.
Where's the sun?
High, high up in the air.

The little black dog ran round the
    house,
And set the bull a-roaring,
And drove the monkey in the boat,
Who set the oars a-rowing,
And scared the cock upon the rock,
Who cracked his throat with crow-
    ing.

137

THE GUINEA-PIG

THERE was a little guinea-pig,
Who, being little, was not big;
He always walked upon his feet,
And never fasted when he eat.

When from a place he ran away,
He never at that place did stay;
And while he ran, as I am told,
He ne'er stood still for young or old.

He often squeaked and sometimes
    vi'lent,
And when he squeaked he ne'er was
    silent;
Though ne'er instructed by a cat,
He knew a mouse was not a rat.

One day, as I am certified,
He took a whim and fairly died;
And as I'm told by men of sense,
He never has been living since.

A TALE

THERE was an old woman sat spin-
    ning,
And that's the first beginning;
She had a calf,
And that's half;
She took it by the tail,
And threw it over the wall,
And that's all.

BABY AND I

BABY and I
Were baked in a pie,
The gravy was wonderful hot.
    We had nothing to pay
    To the baker that day
And so we crept out of the pot.

WHAT CARE I?

WHAT care I how black I be?
Twenty pounds will marry me;
If twenty won't, forty shall,
For I'm my mother's bouncing girl.

TO MR. PUNCHINELLO

OH, mother, I shall be married to
    Mr. Punchinello,
To Mr. Punch,
To Mr. Joe,
To Mr. Nell,
To Mr. Lo,
Mr. Punch, Mr. Joe,
Mr. Nell, Mr. Lo,
To Mr. Punchinello.

THREE AGAINST ONE

OLD Sir Simon the king,
And young Sir Simon the squire,
    And old Mrs. Hickabout
    Kicked Mrs. Kickabout
Round about our coal fire.

WHAT'S THE NEWS?

WHAT's the news of the day,
Good neighbour, I pray?
They say the balloon
Is gone up to the moon.

THREE CHILDREN SLIDING

THREE children sliding on the ice,
  Upon a summer's day,
As it fell out, they all fell in,
  The rest they ran away.

Now had these children been at
    home,
  Or sliding on dry ground,
Ten thousand pounds to one penny
  They had not all been drowned.

You parents all that children have,
  And you that have got none,
If you would have them safe abroad,
  Pray keep them safe at home.

AN OLD WOMAN

THERE was an old woman,
  And what do you think?
She lived upon nothing
  But victuals and drink:
Victuals and drink
  Were the chief of her diet,
And yet this old woman
  Could never keep quiet.

MONEY WORKS WONDERS

WILL you lend me your mare to ride
    but a mile?
No, she is lame leaping over a stile.
Alack! and I must go to the fair,
I'll give you good money for lending
    your mare.
Oho! Say you so?
Money will make the mare to go.

PLAINT

I AM a pretty wench,
  And I come a great way hence,
And sweethearts I can get none:
  But every dirty sow
  Can get sweethearts enough,
And I pretty wench can get none.

THE PHILOSOPHER

As I walked by myself
And talked to myself,
  Myself said unto me,
Look to thyself,
Take care of thyself,
  For nobody cares for thee.

I answered myself,
And said to myself
  In the self-same repartee,
Look to thyself,
Or not to thyself,
  The self-same thing will be.

The Man with Nought

THERE was a man and he had nought,
    And robbers came to rob him;
He crept up to the chimney top,
    And then they thought they had
        him.

But he got down on the other side,
    And then they could not find him;
He ran fourteen miles in fifteen days,
    And never looked behind him.

UNDER A HILL

THERE was an old woman
    Lived under a hill,
And if she's not gone
    She lives there still.

THE TURNIP VENDOR

IF a man who turnips cries,
Cry not when his father dies,
It is proof that he would rather
Have a turnip than his father.

MAN OF THESSALY

THERE was a man of Thessaly
    And he was wondrous wise,
He jumped into a bramble bush
    And scratched out both his eyes.
And when he saw his eyes were out,
    With all his might and main
He jumped into another bush
    And scratched them in again.

A RAT

THERE was a rat, for want
    of stairs,
Went down a rope to say
    his prayers.

TWO COMICAL FOLK

IN a cottage in Fife
    Lived a man and his wife,
Who, believe me, were comical folk;
    For, to people's surprise,
    They both saw with their eyes,
And their tongues moved whenever they spoke.
    When quite fast asleep,
    I've been told that to keep
Their eyes open they could not contrive;
    They walked on their feet,
    And 'twas thought what they eat
Helped, with drinking, to keep them alive.

The Man who Jumped

THERE was a man, he went mad,
He jumped into a paper bag;
The paper bag was too narrow,
He jumped into a wheelbarrow;
The wheelbarrow took on fire,
He jumped into a cow byre;
The cow byre was too nasty,
He jumped into an apple pasty;
The apple pasty was too sweet,
He jumped into Chester-le-Street;
Chester-le-Street was full of stones,
He fell down and broke his bones.

THE PIPER

THERE was a piper had a cow
  And he had nought to give her.
He pulled out his pipes and played
    her a tune,
  And bade the cow consider.

The cow considered very well
  And gave the piper a penny,
And bade him play the other tune,
  'Corn rigs are bonny'.

WHAT's in the cupboard?
Says Mr. Hubbard.
A knuckle of veal,
Says Mr. Beal.
Is that all?
Says Mr. Ball.
And enough too,
Says Mr. Glue;
And away they all flew.

SHORT SONG

THERE was an old crow
  Sat upon a clod;
That's the end of my song.
  —That's odd.

THE WONDER OF WONDERS

I SAW a peacock with a fiery tail
I saw a blazing comet drop down hail
I saw a cloud with ivy curled around
I saw a sturdy oak creep on the ground
I saw an ant swallow up a whale
I saw a raging sea brim full of ale
I saw a Venice glass sixteen foot deep
I saw a well full of men's tears that weep
I saw their eyes all in a flame of fire
I saw a house high as the moon and higher
I saw the sun at twelve o'clock at night
I saw the man who saw this wondrous sight.

141

DOCTOR FOSTER

OLD Doctor Foster
Went to Gloucester
To preach the word of God;
  When he came there,
  He sat in a chair,
And gave all the people a nod.

PIG SHAVING

BARBER, barber, shave a pig,
How many hairs will make a wig?
Four and twenty, that's enough.
Give the barber a pinch of snuff.

THE PRIEST OF FELTON

THE little priest of Felton,
The little priest of Felton,
He killed a mouse within his house,
And nobody there to help him.

ON OATH

  As I went to Bonner,
    I met a pig
    Without a wig,
  Upon my word and honour.

CLOSE SHAVE

THE barber shaved the mason,
  As I suppose,
  Cut off his nose,
And popped it in a basin.

WASHING UP

WHEN I was a little boy
I washed my mammy's dishes;
I put my finger in my eye,
And pulled out golden fishes.

ANNA ELISE

ANNA Elise
She jumped with surprise;
The surprise was so quick,
It played her a trick;
The trick was so rare,
She jumped in a chair;
The chair was so frail,
She jumped in a pail;
The pail was so wet,
She jumped in a net;
The net was so small,
She jumped on a ball;
The ball was so round,
She jumped on the ground;
And ever since then
    she's been turning around.

PREVARICATION

NOSE, nose,
  Jolly red nose,
And what gave thee
  That jolly red nose?
Nutmeg and ginger,
  Cinnamon and cloves,
That's what gave me
  This jolly red nose.

GRINDING

My mill grinds pepper and spice;
Your mill grinds rats and mice.

HYDER IDDLE

Hyder iddle diddle dell,
A yard of pudding's not an ell;
Not forgetting tweedle-dye,
A tailor's goose will never fly.

BARNEY BODKIN

Barney Bodkin broke his nose,
Without feet we can't have toes;
Crazy folks are always mad,
Want of money makes us sad.

IN THE DUMPS

We are all in the dumps,
For diamonds are trumps,
The kittens are gone to St. Paul's.
The babies are bit,
The moon's in a fit,
And the houses are built without
walls.

PETER WHITE

Peter White will ne'er go right;
Would you know the reason why?
He follows his nose wherever
he goes,
And that stands all awry.

JACKY JINGLE

Now what do you think
Of little Jack Jingle?
Before he was married
He used to live single.
But after he married,
To alter his life,
He left off living single
And lived with his wife.

BUZZ AND HUM

Buzz, quoth the blue fly,
Hum, quoth the bee,
Buzz and hum they cry,
And so do we:
In his ear, in his nose,
Thus do you see,
He ate the dormouse,
Else it was thee.

UP TIME

Awake, arise,
Pull out your eyes,
And hear what time of day;
And when you have done,
Pull out your tongue,
And see what you can say.

BOUNCE BUCKRAM

Bounce, buckram, velvet's dear,
Christmas comes but once a year;
When it comes it brings good cheer,
But when it's gone it's never near.

A MAN in the wilderness asked me,
How many strawberries grow in the
    sea.
I answered him, as I thought good,
As many red herrings as swim in the
    wood.

MOTHER, may I go out to swim?
    Yes, my darling daughter.
Hang your clothes on a hickory limb
    And don't go near the water.

THERE WAS A MONKEY

THERE was a monkey climbed a tree,
When he fell down, then down fell he.

There was a crow sat on a stone,
When he was gone, then there was none.

There was an old wife did eat an apple,
When she ate two, she ate a couple.

There was a horse going to the mill,
When he went on, he stood not still.

There was a butcher cut his thumb,
When it did bleed, then blood did come.

There was a lackey ran a race,
When he ran fast, he ran apace.

There was a cobbler clouting shoon,
When they were mended, they were done.

There was a navy went to Spain,
When it returned it came again.

AND THAT'S ALL

THERE was an old man,
And he had a calf,
    And that's half;
He took him out of the stall,
And put him on the wall,
    And that's all.

RIDDLES

HARD NUTS TO CRACK

Riddles

RIDDLE me, riddle me ree,
A little man in a tree;
A stick in his hand,
A stone in his throat,
If you read me this riddle
I'll give you a groat.

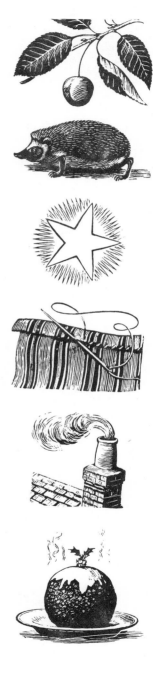

LITTLE Billy Breek
Sits by the reek,
He has more horns
Than all the king's sheep.

HIGHER than a house,
Higher than a tree;
Oh, whatever can that be?

OLD Mother Twitchett has but one eye,
And a long tail which she can let fly,
And every time she goes over a gap,
She leaves a bit of her tail in a trap.

BLACK within, and red without,
Four corners round about.

FLOUR of England, fruit of Spain,
Met together in a shower of rain;
Put in a bag, tied round with a string;
If you tell me this riddle,
I'll give you a ring.

Riddles

Arthur O'Bower has broken his band,
He comes roaring up the land;
The King of Scots, with all his power,
Cannot turn Arthur of the Bower.

In Spring I look gay,
Decked in comely array,
In Summer more clothing I wear;
When colder it grows,
I fling off my clothes,
And in Winter quite naked appear.

Two bodies have I,
Though both joined in one.
The stiller I stand,
The faster I run.

Clothed in yellow, red, and green,
I prate before the king and queen;
Of neither house nor land possessed,
By lords and knights I am caressed.

Formed long ago, yet made today,
Employed while others sleep;
What few would like to give away,
Nor any wish to keep.

As round as an apple,
As deep as a cup,
And all the king's horses
Cannot pull it up.

Riddles

As black as ink and isn't ink,
As white as milk and isn't milk,
As soft as silk and isn't silk,
And hops about like a filly-foal.

Two brothers we are,
Great burdens we bear,
On which we are bitterly pressed;
The truth is to say,
We are full all the day,
And empty when we go to rest.

As I was going o'er Tipple Tine,
I met a flock of bonny swine;
Some yellow necked,
Some yellow backed,
They were the very bonniest swine
That ever went over Tipple Tine.

Long legs, crooked thighs,
Little head, and no eyes.

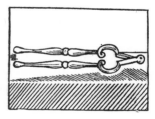

As I was walking in a field of wheat,
I picked up something good to eat;
Neither fish, flesh, fowl, nor bone,
I kept it till it ran alone.

Purple, yellow, red, and green,
The king cannot reach it, nor yet the queen;
Nor can Old Noll, whose power's so great:
Tell me this riddle while I count eight.

Riddles

A RIDDLE, a riddle,
As I suppose;
A hundred eyes,
And never a nose.

BLACK I am and much admired,
Men seek for me until they're tired;
When they find me, break my head,
And take me from my resting bed.

HITTY Pitty within the wall,
Hitty Pitty without the wall;
If you touch Hitty Pitty,
Hitty Pitty will bite you.

HE went to the wood and caught it,
He sat him down and sought it;
Because he could not find it,
Home with him he brought it.

As I was going o'er London Bridge,
I heard something crack;
Not a man in all England
Can mend that.

As soft as silk,
As white as milk,
As bitter as gall;
A thick wall,
And a green coat covers me all.

Riddles

Hoddy doddy,
With a round black body,
Three feet and a wooden hat.
Pray tell me, what is that?

Highty, tighty, paradighty,
Clothed all in green,
The king could not read it,
No more could the queen;
They sent for the wise men
From out of the East,
Who said it had horns,
But was not a beast.

A house full, a hole full,
And you cannot gather a bowl full.

I have a little sister, they call her
    Peep-Peep,
She wades the waters deep, deep, deep;
She climbs the mountains high, high,
    high;
Poor little creature she has but one eye.

Thirty white horses
Upon a red hill,
Now they stamp,
Now they champ,
Now they stand still.

Two legs sat upon three legs
With one leg in his lap;
In comes four legs
And runs away with one leg;
Up jumps two legs,
Catches up three legs,
Throws it after four legs,
And makes him bring back one leg.

Riddles

The land was white,
  The seed was black;
It will take a good scholar
  To riddle me that.

A SHOEMAKER makes shoes without leather,
With all the four elements put together,
Fire, Water, Earth, Air,
And every customer takes two pair.

As round as an apple,
  As deep as a pail;
It never cries out
  Till it's caught by the tail.

In marble walls as white as milk,
Lined with a skin as soft as silk,
Within a fountain crystal-clear,
A golden apple doth appear.
No doors there are to this stronghold,
Yet thieves break in and steal the gold.

Goes through the mud,
And through the mud,
And only leaves one track.

Around the rick, around the rick,
And there I found my Uncle Dick.
I screwed his neck,
I sucked his blood,
And left his body lying.

Riddles

I'M called by the name of a man,
Yet am as little as a mouse;
When winter comes I love to be
With my red target near the house.

  FOUR stiff-standers,
  Four dilly-danders,
  Two lookers,
  Two crookers,
  And a wig-wag.

  WHITE bird featherless
  Flew from Paradise,
Pitched on the castle wall;
  Along came Lord Landless,
  Took it up handless,
And rode away horseless
    to the King's white hall.

THERE was a thing a full month old
  When Adam was no more;
Before the thing was five weeks old
  Adam was years four score.

LITTLE bird of paradise,
She works her work both neat and nice;
She pleases God, she pleases man,
She does the work that no man can.

LITTLE Nancy Etticoat,
With a white petticoat,
And a red nose;
She has no feet or hands,
The longer she stands
The shorter she grows.

153

Come Riddle Me Riddle Me Riddle Me Ree

HICK-A-MORE, Hack-a-more,
Hung on a kitchen door;
　Nothing so long,
　And nothing so strong,
As Hick-a-more, Hack-a-more,
Hung on the kitchen door.

[A sunbeam]

ELIZABETH, Elspeth, Betsy, and Bess,
They all went together to seek a
　bird's nest;
They found a bird's nest with five
　eggs in,
They all took one, and left four in.

As I was going to St. Ives,
I met a man with seven wives;
Each wife had seven sacks,
Each sack had seven cats,
Each cat had seven kits:
Kits, cats, sacks, and wives,
How many were there going to St.
　Ives?

[One or None]

THERE was a man who had no eyes,
He went abroad to view the skies;
He saw a tree with apples on it,
He took no apples off, yet left no
　apples on it.

[The man, who was one-eyed, took one of
the two apples, which were all there were
on the tree]

WHAT God never sees,
What the king seldom sees,
What we see every day;
Read my riddle, I pray.

[An equal]

HIDDEN NAMES

As I was a-walking on Westminster
　Bridge,
I met with a Westminster scholar;
He pulled off his cap, *an' drew* off
　his gloves,
Now what was the name of this
　scholar?

THERE was a girl in our town,
Silk *an'* satin was her gown,
Silk *an'* satin, gold *an'* velvet,
Guess her name, three times I've
　telled it.

THERE was a king met a king
　In a narrow lane;
Says this king to that king,
　Where have you been?
I have been a-hunting
　The buck and the doe.
Will you lend me your dog,
　That I may do so?
There's the dog, *take* the dog.
　What's the dog's name?
I've told you already
　And won't tell you again.

THERE *was* a man rode through our
　town,
Gray Grizzle *was* his name;
His saddle-bow *was* gilt and gold,
　Three times I've named his name.

None Are So Blind As They That Won't See

THERE were three sisters in a hall,
There came a knight amongst them
  all;
Good morrow, aunt, to the one,
Good morrow, aunt, to the other,
Good morrow, gentlewoman, to the
  third,
  If you were aunt,
    As the other two be,
  I would say good morrow,
    Then, aunts, all three.

[The third sister was his mother]

SEE, see, what shall I see?
A horse's head where his tail should
  be.

PUNCTUATE

EVERY lady in this land
Has twenty nails upon each hand
Five and twenty on hands and feet
All this is true without deceit.

KING Charles the First walked and
  talked
Half an hour after his head was cut
  off.

THE fiddler and his wife,
  The piper and his mother,
Ate three half cakes, three whole
  cakes,
  And three-quarters of another.

[If the fiddler's wife was the piper's
mother the division was not difficult]

CONSTRUE

  INFIR taris,
  Inoak noneis,
  Inmud eelsare,
  Inclay noneare.
  Goatseativy;
  Mareseatoats.

TWELVE pears hanging high,
Twelve knights riding by;
Each knight took a pear,
And yet left eleven there.

[Perhaps only Sir *Eachknight* took one]

CHARADE

HIGGLEDY-PIGGLEDY here we lie,
Picked and plucked and put in a pie.
My first is snapping, snarling,
  growling,
My second's industrious, romping,
  and prowling.
Higgledy-piggledy here we lie,
Picked and plucked and put in a pie.

[Currants]

MAKE three-fourths of a cross,
  And a circle complete,
And let two semicircles
  On a perpendicular meet;
Next add a triangle
  That stands on two feet;
Next two semicircles
  And a circle complete.

[TOBACCO]

Tongue Trippers

BETTY Botter bought some butter,
But, she said, the butter's bitter;
If I put it in my batter
It will make my batter bitter,
But a bit of better butter,
That would make my batter better.
So she bought a bit of butter
Better than her bitter butter,
And she put it in her batter
And the batter was not bitter.
So t'was better Betty Botter
Bought a bit of better butter.

MOSES supposes his toeses are roses,
But Moses supposes erroneously;
For nobody's toeses are posies of
    roses
As Moses supposes his toeses to be.

THREE crooked cripples went through
    Cripplegate,
And through Cripplegate went three
    crooked cripples.

I NEED not your needles,
They're needless to me,
For kneading of needles
Were needless, you see;
But did my neat trousers
But need to be kneed,
I then should have need
Of your needles indeed.

THREE grey geese in a green field
    grazing,
Grey were the geese and green was
    the grazing.

PETER Piper picked a peck of pickled
    pepper;
A peck of pickled pepper Peter Piper
    picked.
If Peter Piper picked a peck of
    pickled pepper,
Where's the peck of pickled pepper
    Peter Piper picked?

MY dame hath a lame tame crane,
My dame hath a crane that is lame.
Pray, gentle Jane, let my dame's
    tame crane
Feed and come home again.

My grandmother sent me a new-fashioned three-cornered
    cambric country-cut handkerchief.
Not an old-fashioned three-cornered cambric country-cut
    handkerchief,
But a new-fashioned three-cornered cambric country-cut
    handkerchief.

The Leith police dismisseth us,
I'm thankful, sir, to say;
The Leith police dismisseth us,
They thought we sought to stay.
The Leith police dismisseth us,
We both sighed sighs apiece,
And the sigh that we sighed as we
said goodbye
Was the size of the Leith police.

A thatcher of Thatchwood went to
Thatchet a-thatching;
Did a thatcher of Thatchwood go to
Thatchet a-thatching?
If a thatcher of Thatchwood went
to Thatchet a-thatching,
Where's the thatching the thatcher
of Thatchwood has thatched?

Swan swam over the sea,
Swim, swan, swim!
Swan swam back again,
Well swum swan!

Theophilus Thistledown, the suc-
cessful thistle sifter,
In sifting a sieve of unsifted thistles,
Thrust three thousand thistles
Through the thick of his thumb.
If, then, Theophilus Thistledown, the
successful thistle sifter,
In sifting a sieve full of unsifted
thistles,
Thrust three thousand thistles
Through the thick of his thumb,
See that thou, in sifting a sieve of
unsifted thistles,
Do not get the unsifted thistles
stuck in thy tongue.

Robert Rowley rolled a round roll
round,
A round roll Robert Rowley rolled
round;
Where rolled the round roll
Robert Rowley rolled round?

When a Twister a-twisting will
twist him a twist,
For the twisting of his twist, he
three twines doth intwist;
But if one of the twines of the twist
do untwist,
The twine that untwisteth, un-
twisteth the twist.

Untwirling the twine that untwisteth
between,
He twirls, with his twister, the two
in a twine;
Then twice having twisted the
twines of the twine,
He twitcheth, the twice he had
twined, in twain.

The twain that, in twining, before
in the twine
As twines were intwisted; he now
doth untwine;
Twixt the twain inter-twisting a
twine more between,
He, twirling his twister, makes a
twist of the twine.

Round and round the rugged rock
The ragged rascal ran.
How many R's are there in *that?*
Now tell me if you can.

Timothy Titus took two ties
To tie two tups to two tall trees,
To terrify the terrible Thomas a
Tullamees.
How many T's in *that?*

Pease porridge hot, pease porridge cold,
Pease porridge in the pot nine days old.
Spell me *that* without a P,
And a clever scholar you will be.

BALLADS
AND
SONGS

THE THREE JOVIAL WELSHMEN

THERE were three jovial Welshmen,
 As I have heard men say,
And they would go a-hunting
 Upon St. David's Day.

All the day they hunted
 And nothing could they find,
But a ship a-sailing,
 A-sailing with the wind.

One said it was a ship,
 The other he said, Nay;
The third said it was a house,
 With the chimney blown away.

And all the night they hunted
 And nothing could they find,
But the moon a-gliding,
 A-gliding with the wind.

One said it was the moon,
 The other he said, Nay;
The third said it was a cheese,
 And half of it cut away.

And all the day they hunted
 And nothing could they find,
But a hedgehog in a bramble bush,
 And that they left behind.

The first said it was a hedgehog,
 The second he said, Nay;
The third said it was a pincushion,
 And the pins stuck in wrong way.

And all the night they hunted
 And nothing could they find,
But a hare in a turnip field,
 And that they left behind.

The first said it was a hare,
 The second he said, Nay;
The third said it was a calf,
 And the cow had run away.

And all the day they hunted
 And nothing could they find,
But an owl in a holly tree,
 And that they left behind.

One said it was an owl,
 The other he said, Nay;
The third said 'twas an old man,
 And his beard growing grey.

* *   * *

THE SURPRISING HISTORY OF
Aiken Drum

THERE was a man lived in the moon, lived in the moon, lived in the moon,
There was a man lived in the moon,
And his name was Aiken Drum;
      And he played upon a ladle, a ladle, a ladle,
      And he played upon a ladle,
      And his name was Aiken Drum.

And his hat was made of good cream cheese, good cream cheese, good cream
    cheese,
And his hat was made of good cream cheese,
And his name was Aiken Drum.

And his coat was made of good roast beef, good roast beef, good roast beef,
And his coat was made of good roast beef,
And his name was Aiken Drum.

And his buttons were made of penny loaves, penny loaves, penny loaves,
And his buttons were made of penny loaves,
And his name was Aiken Drum.

His waistcoat was made of crust of pies, crust of pies, crust of pies,
His waistcoat was made of crust of pies,
And his name was Aiken Drum.

His breeches were made of haggis bags, haggis bags, haggis bags,
His breeches were made of haggis bags,
And his name was Aiken Drum.

* *   * *

AND THE ALMOST OMNIVOROUS

Willy Wood

There was a man in another town, another town, another town,
There was a man in another town,
And his name was Willy Wood;
    And he played upon a razor, a razor, a razor,
    And he played upon a razor,
    And his name was Willy Wood.

And he ate up all the good cream cheese, good cream cheese, good cream
    cheese,
And he ate up all the good cream cheese,
And his name was Willy Wood.

And he ate up all the good roast beef, good roast beef, good roast beef,
And he ate up all the good roast beef,
And his name was Willy Wood.

And he ate up all the penny loaves, penny loaves, penny loaves,
And he ate up all the penny loaves,
And his name was Willy Wood.

And he ate up all the good pie crust, good pie crust, good pie crust,
And he ate up all the good pie crust,
And his name was Willy Wood.

But he choked upon the haggis bags, haggis bags, haggis bags,
But he choked upon the haggis bags,
And that ended Willy Wood.

Tom, the Piper's Son

With all the fun
That he has done

Tom, he was a piper's son,
He learned to play when he was
   young,
But all the tunes that he could
   play
Was, 'Over the hills and far
   away'.
   Over the hills and a great way off,
   The wind shall blow my top-knot off.

Tom with his pipe made such
   a noise,
That he pleased both the girls and
   boys;
They all danced while he did
   play,
   'Over the hills and far away'.
Over the hills and a great way off,
The wind shall blow my top-knot off.

Tom with his pipe did play with
   such skill
That those who heard him could
   never keep still;
As soon as he played they began
   for to dance,
Even pigs on their hind legs
   would after him prance.
   Over the hills and a great way off,
   The wind shall blow my top-knot off.

As Dolly was milking her cow
one day,
Tom took his pipe and began for
to play;
So Doll and the cow danced 'The
Cheshire Round',
Till the pail was broken and the
milk ran on the ground.
  Over the hills and a great way off,
  The wind shall blow my top-knot off.

He met old Dame Trot with a
basket of eggs,
He used his pipe and she used
her legs;
She danced about till the eggs
were all broke,
She began for to fret, but he
laughed at the joke.
  Over the hills and a great way off,
  The wind shall blow my top-knot off.

Tom saw a cross fellow was
beating an ass,
Heavy laden with pots, pans,
dishes, and glass;
He took out his pipe and he
played them a tune,
And the poor donkey's load was
lightened full soon.
  Over the hills and a great way off,
  The wind shall blow my top-knot off.

165

Death and Burial of Cock Robin

WHO killed Cock Robin?
　I, said the Sparrow,
　　With my bow and arrow,
I killed Cock Robin.

Who saw him die?
　I, said the Fly,
　　With my little eye,
I saw him die.

Who caught his blood?
　I, said the Fish,
　　With my little dish,
I caught his blood.

Who'll make his shroud?
　I, said the Beetle,
　　With my thread and needle,
I'll make the shroud.

Who'll dig his grave?
　I, said the Owl,
　　With my pick and shovel,
I'll dig his grave.

Who'll be the parson?
  I, said the Rook,
  With my little book,
I'll be the parson.

Who'll be the clerk?
  I, said the Lark,
  If it's not in the dark,
I'll be the clerk.

Who'll carry the link?
  I, said the Linnet,
  I'll fetch it in a minute,
I'll carry the link.

Who'll be chief mourner?
  I, said the Dove,
  I mourn for my love,
I'll be chief mourner.

Who'll carry the coffin?
  I, said the Kite,
  If it's not through the night,
I'll carry the coffin.

Who'll bear the pall?
  We, said the Wren,
  Both the cock and the hen,
We'll bear the pall.

Who'll sing a psalm?
  I, said the Thrush,
  As she sat on a bush,
I'll sing a psalm.

Who'll toll the bell?
  I, said the Bull,
  Because I can pull,
So Cock Robin, farewell.

All the birds of the air
  Fell a-sighing and a-sobbing,
When they heard the bell toll
  For poor Cock Robin.

NOTICE
To all it concerns,
  This notice apprises,
The Sparrow's for trial
  At next bird assizes.

THE LITTLE WOMAN AND THE PEDLAR

There was a little woman,
  As I have heard tell,
She went to market
  Her eggs for to sell;
She went to market
  All on a market day,
And she fell asleep
  On the king's highway.

There came by a pedlar,
  His name was Stout,
He cut her petticoats
  All round about;
He cut her petticoats
  Up to her knees;
Which made the little woman
  To shiver and sneeze.

When this little woman
  Began to awake,
She began to shiver,
  And she began to shake;
She began to shake,
  And she began to cry,
Lawk a mercy on me,
  This is none of I!

But if this be I,
  As I do hope it be,
I have a little dog at home
  And he knows me;
If it be I,
  He'll wag his little tail,
And if it be not I
  He'll loudly bark and wail!

Home went the little woman
  All in the dark,
Up starts the little dog,
  And he began to bark;
He began to bark,
  And she began to cry,
Lawk a mercy on me,
  This is none of I!

MOUSE AND MOUSER

WHAT are you doing, my lady, my lady,
What are you doing, my lady?

I'm spinning old breeches, good body, good body,
I'm spinning old breeches, good body.

Long may you wear them, my lady, my lady,
Long may you wear them, my lady.

I'll wear 'em and tear 'em, good body, good body,
I'll wear 'em and tear 'em, good body.

I was sweeping my room, my lady, my lady,
I was sweeping my room, my lady.

The cleaner you'd be, good body, good body,
The cleaner you'd be, good body.

I found me a sixpence, my lady, my lady,
I found me a sixpence, my lady.

The richer you were, good body, good body,
The richer you were, good body.

I went to the market, my lady, my lady,
I went to the market, my lady.

The further you went, good body, good body,
The further you went, good body.

I bought me a pudding, my lady, my lady,
I bought me a pudding, my lady.

The more meat you had, good body, good body,
The more meat you had, good body.

I put it in the window to cool, my lady,
I put it in the window to cool.

The faster you'd eat it, good body, good body,
The faster you'd eat it, good body.

The cat came and ate it, my lady, my lady,
The cat came and ate it, my lady.

And I'll eat you too, good body, good body,
And I'll eat you too, good body.

DILLY DILLY

Oh, what have you got for dinner, Mrs. Bond?
There's beef in the larder, and ducks in the pond;
Dilly, dilly, dilly, dilly, come to be killed,
For you must be stuffed and my customers filled!

Send us the beef first, good Mrs. Bond,
And get us some ducks dressed out of the pond,
Cry, Dilly, dilly, dilly, dilly, come to be killed,
For you must be stuffed and my customers filled!

John Ostler, go fetch me a duckling or two.
Ma'am, says John Ostler, I'll try what I can do.
Cry, Dilly, dilly, dilly, dilly, come to be killed,
For you must be stuffed and my customers filled!

I have been to the ducks that swim in the pond,
But I found they won't come to be killed, Mrs. Bond;
I cried, Dilly, dilly, dilly, dilly, come to be killed,
For you must be stuffed and my customers filled!

Mrs. Bond she flew down to the pond in a rage,
With plenty of onions and plenty of sage;
She cried, Dilly, dilly, dilly, dilly, come to be killed,
For you must be stuffed and my customers filled!

She cried, Little wag-tails, come and be killed,
For you must be stuffed and my customers filled!
Dilly, dilly, dilly, dilly, come to be killed,
For you must be stuffed and my customers filled!

THE LOVE-SICK FROG

A FROG he would a-wooing go,
  Heigh ho! says Rowley,
Whether his mother would let him or no.
   With a rowley, powley, gammon and spinach,
   Heigh ho! says Anthony Rowley.

So off he set with his opera hat,
  Heigh ho! says Rowley,
And on the road he met with a rat.
   With a rowley, powley, gammon and spinach,
   Heigh ho! says Anthony Rowley.

Pray, Mister Rat, will you go with me?
  Heigh ho! says Rowley,
Kind Mistress Mousey for to see?
   With a rowley, powley, gammon and spinach,
   Heigh ho! says Anthony Rowley.

They came to the door of Mousey's hall,
  Heigh ho! says Rowley,
They gave a loud knock, and they gave a loud call.
   With a rowley, powley, gammon and spinach,
   Heigh ho! says Anthony Rowley.

Pray, Mistress Mouse, are you within?
  Heigh ho! says Rowley,
Oh yes, kind sirs, I'm sitting to spin.
  With a rowley, powley, gammon and spinach,
  Heigh ho! says Anthony Rowley.

Pray, Mistress Mouse, will you give us some beer?
  Heigh ho! says Rowley,
For Froggy and I are fond of good cheer.
  With a rowley, powley, gammon and spinach,
  Heigh ho! says Anthony Rowley.

Pray, Mister Frog, will you give us a song?
  Heigh ho! says Rowley,
Let it be something that's not very long.
  With a rowley, powley, gammon and spinach,
  Heigh ho! says Anthony Rowley.

Indeed, Mistress Mouse, replied Mister Frog,
  Heigh ho! says Rowley,
A cold has made me as hoarse as a dog.
  With a rowley, powley, gammon and spinach,
  Heigh ho! says Anthony Rowley.

Since you have a cold, Mister Frog, Mousey said,
  Heigh ho! says Rowley,
I'll sing you a song that I have just made.
  With a rowley, powley, gammon and spinach,
  Heigh ho! says Anthony Rowley.

But while they were all a-merry-making,
  Heigh ho! says Rowley,
A cat and her kittens came tumbling in.
  With a rowley, powley, gammon and spinach,
  Heigh ho! says Anthony Rowley.

The cat she seized the rat by the crown,
    Heigh ho! says Rowley,
The kittens they pulled the little mouse down.
    With a rowley, powley, gammon and spinach,
    Heigh ho! says Anthony Rowley.

This put Mister Frog in a terrible fright,
    Heigh ho! says Rowley,
He took up his hat and he wished them good-night.
    With a rowley, powley, gammon and spinach,
    Heigh ho! says Anthony Rowley.

But as Froggy was crossing over a brook,
    Heigh ho! says Rowley,
A lily-white duck came and gobbled him up.
    With a rowley, powley, gammon and spinach,
    Heigh ho! says Anthony Rowley.

So there was an end of one, two, three,
    Heigh ho! says Rowley,
The rat, the mouse, and the little frog-ee.
    With a rowley, powley, gammon and spinach,
    Heigh ho! says Anthony Rowley.

ROGER AND DOLLY

Young Roger came tapping at Dolly's window,
    Thumpaty, thumpaty, thump.
He begged for admittance, she answered him, No,
    Frumpaty, frumpaty, frump.
No, no, Roger, no, as you came you may go,
    Stumpaty, stumpaty, stump.

THE MILK MAID

WHERE are you going to, my pretty maid?
I'm going a-milking, sir, she said,
Sir, she said, sir, she said,
I'm going a-milking, sir, she said.

May I go with you, my pretty maid?
You're kindly welcome, sir, she said,
Sir, she said, sir, she said,
You're kindly welcome, sir, she said.

Say, will you marry me, my pretty maid?
Yes, if you please, kind sir, she said,
Sir, she said, sir, she said,
Yes, if you please, kind sir, she said.

What is your father, my pretty maid?
My father's a farmer, sir, she said,
Sir, she said, sir, she said,
My father's a farmer, sir, she said.

What is your fortune, my pretty maid?
My face is my fortune, sir, she said,
Sir, she said, sir, she said,
My face is my fortune, sir, she said.

Then I can't marry you, my pretty maid.
Nobody asked you, sir, she said,
Sir, she said, sir, she said,
Nobody asked you, sir, she said.

THE LITTLE MAN AND THE LITTLE MAID

THERE was a little man,
And he wooed a little maid,
And he said, Little maid, will you wed, wed, wed?
I have little more to say,
Than will you, yea or nay?
For the least said is soonest mended, ded, ded.

Then this little maid she said,
Little sir, you've little said,
To induce a little maid for to wed, wed, wed;
You must say a little more,
And produce a little ore,
Ere I to the church will be led, led, led.

Then the little man replied,
If you'll be my little bride,
I will raise my love notes a little higher, higher, higher;
Though I little love to prate
You will find my heart is great,
With the little God of Love all on fire, fire, fire.

Then the little maid replied,
If I should be your bride,
Pray, what must we have for to eat, eat, eat?
Will the flames that you're so rich in
Make a fire in the kitchen,
And the little God of Love turn the spit, spit, spit?

Then the little man he sighed,
And some say a little cried,
And his little heart was big with sorrow, sorrow, sorrow;
I'll be your little slave,
And if the little that I have,
Be too little, little dear, I will borrow, borrow, borrow.

Then the little man so gent,
Made the little maid relent,
And set her little soul a-thinking, king, king;
Though his little was but small,
Yet she had his little all,
And could have of a cat but her skin, skin, skin.

A MELANCHOLY SONG

TRIP upon trenchers, and dance upon dishes,
My mother sent me for some barm, some barm;
She bid me tread lightly, and come again quickly,
For fear the young men should do me some harm.
    Yet didn't you see, yet didn't you see,
    What naughty tricks they put upon me:
        They broke my pitcher,
        And spilt the water,
        And huffed my mother,
        And chid her daughter,
    And kissed my sister instead of me.

177

THE WREN HUNT

WE will go to the wood, says Robin to Bobbin,
We will go to the wood, says Richard to Robin,
We will go to the wood, says John all alone,
We will go to the wood, says everyone.

What to do there? says Robin to Bobbin,
What to do there? says Richard to Robin,
What to do there? says John all alone,
What to do there? says everyone.

We'll shoot at a wren, says Robin to Bobbin,
We'll shoot at a wren, says Richard to Robin,
We'll shoot at a wren, says John all alone,
We'll shoot at a wren, says everyone.

She's down, she's down, says Robin to Bobbin,
She's down, she's down, says Richard to Robin,
She's down, she's down, says John all alone,
She's down, she's down, says everyone.

Then pounce, then pounce, says Robin to Bobbin,
Then pounce, then pounce, says Richard to Robin,
Then pounce, then pounce, says John all alone,
Then pounce, then pounce, says everyone.

She is dead, she is dead, says Robin to Bobbin,
She is dead, she is dead, says Richard to Robin,
She is dead, she is dead, says John all alone,
She is dead, she is dead, says everyone.

How get her home? says Robin to Bobbin,
How get her home? says Richard to Robin,
How get her home? says John all alone,
How get her home? says everyone.

In a cart with six horses, says Robin to Bobbin,
In a cart with six horses, says Richard to Robin,
In a cart with six horses, says John all alone,
In a cart with six horses, says everyone.

Then hoist, boys, hoist, says Robin to Bobbin,
Then hoist, boys, hoist, says Richard to Robin,
Then hoist, boys, hoist, says John all alone,
Then hoist, boys, hoist, says everyone.

How shall we dress her? says Robin to Bobbin,
How shall we dress her? says Richard to Robin,
How shall we dress her? says John all alone,
How shall we dress her? says everyone.

We'll hire seven cooks, says Robin to Bobbin,
We'll hire seven cooks, says Richard to Robin,
We'll hire seven cooks, says John all alone,
We'll hire seven cooks, says everyone.

How shall we boil her? says Robin to Bobbin,
How shall we boil her? says Richard to Robin,
How shall we boil her? says John all alone,
How shall we boil her? says everyone.

In the brewer's big pan, says Robin to Bobbin,
In the brewer's big pan, says Richard to Robin,
In the brewer's big pan, says John all alone,
In the brewer's big pan, says everyone.

THE PLOUGHBOY IN LUCK

My father he died, but I can't tell you how,
He left me six horses to drive in my plough:
　　With a whim, wham, wabble ho!
　　Jack's lost his saddle oh!
　　Blossy boys, bubble oh!
　　Over the brow.

I sold my six horses and bought me a cow,
I'd fain have made a fortune, but didn't know how:
　　With a whim, wham, wabble ho!
　　Jack's lost his saddle oh!
　　Blossy boys, bubble oh!
　　Over the brow.

I sold my cow and bought me a calf,
I never made a bargain but I lost the better half:
　　With a whim, wham, wabble ho!
　　Jack's lost his saddle oh!
　　Blossy boys, bubble oh!
　　Over the brow.

I sold my calf and bought me a cat,
To lie down before the fire and warm its little back:
　　With a whim, wham, wabble ho!
　　Jack's lost his saddle oh!
　　Blossy boys, bubble oh!
　　Over the brow.

I sold my cat and bought me a mouse,
But she fired her tail and burnt down my house:
　　With a whim, wham, wabble ho!
　　Jack's lost his saddle oh!
　　Blossy boys, bubble oh!
　　Over the brow.

LOVE SONG

LAVENDER's blue, diddle, diddle,
    Lavender's green;
When I am king, diddle, diddle,
    You shall be queen.

Who told you so, diddle, diddle,
    Who told you so?
'Twas mine own heart, diddle, diddle,
    That told me so.

Call up your men, diddle, diddle,
    Set them to work,
Some to the plough, diddle, diddle,
    Some to the fork.

Some to make hay, diddle, diddle,
    Some to reap corn,
Whilst you and I, diddle, diddle,
    Keep the bed warm.

Roses are red, diddle, diddle,
    Violets are blue;
Because you love me, diddle, diddle,
    I will love you.

Let the birds sing, diddle, diddle,
    And the lambs play;
We shall be safe, diddle, diddle,
    Out of harm's way.

DID YOU SEE MY WIFE?

DID you see my wife, did you see, did you see,
    Did you see my wife looking for me?
She wears a straw bonnet, with white ribbands on it,
    And dimity petticoats over her knee.

A FARMYARD SONG

I HAD a cat and the cat pleased me,
I fed my cat by yonder tree;
    Cat goes fiddle-i-fee.

I had a hen and the hen pleased me,
I fed my hen by yonder tree;
    Hen goes chimmy-chuck, chimmy-chuck,
    Cat goes fiddle-i-fee.

I had a duck and the duck pleased me,
I fed my duck by yonder tree;
    Duck goes quack, quack,
    Hen goes chimmy-chuck, chimmy-chuck,
    Cat goes fiddle-i-fee.

I had a goose and the goose pleased me,
I fed my goose by yonder tree;
    Goose goes swishy, swashy,
    Duck goes quack, quack,
    Hen goes chimmy-chuck, chimmy-chuck,
    Cat goes fiddle-i-fee.

I had a sheep and the sheep pleased me,
I fed my sheep by yonder tree;
    Sheep goes baa, baa,
    Goose goes swishy, swashy,
    Duck goes quack, quack,
    Hen goes chimmy-chuck, chimmy-chuck, ,
    Cat goes fiddle-i-fee.

I had a pig and the pig pleased me,
I fed my pig by yonder tree;
    Pig goes griffy, gruffy,
    Sheep goes baa, baa,
    Goose goes swishy, swashy,
    Duck goes quack, quack,
    Hen goes chimmy-chuck, chimmy-chuck,
    Cat goes fiddle-i-fee.

I had a cow and the cow pleased me,
I fed my cow by yonder tree;
    Cow goes moo, moo,
    Pig goes griffy, gruffy,
    Sheep goes baa, baa,
    Goose goes swishy, swashy,
    Duck goes quack, quack,
    Hen goes chimmy-chuck, chimmy-chuck,
    Cat goes fiddle-i-fee.

I had a horse and the horse pleased me,
I fed my horse by yonder tree;
    Horse goes neigh, neigh,
    Cow goes moo, moo,
    Pig goes griffy, gruffy,
    Sheep goes baa, baa,
    Goose goes swishy, swashy,
    Duck goes quack, quack,
    Hen goes chimmy-chuck, chimmy-chuck,
    Cat goes fiddle-i-fee.

I had a dog and the dog pleased me,
I fed my dog by yonder tree;
    Dog goes bow-wow, bow-wow,
    Horse goes neigh, neigh,
    Cow goes moo, moo,
    Pig goes griffy, gruffy,
    Sheep goes baa, baa,
    Goose goes swishy, swashy,
    Duck goes quack, quack,
    Hen goes chimmy-chuck, chimmy-chuck,
    Cat goes fiddle-i-fee.

The Jolly Tester

I LOVE sixpence, jolly little sixpence,
   I love sixpence better than my life;
I spent a penny of it, I lent a penny of it,
   And I took fourpence home to my wife.

Oh, my little fourpence, jolly little fourpence,
   I love fourpence better than my life;
I spent a penny of it, I lent a penny of it,
   And I took twopence home to my wife.

Oh, my little twopence, jolly little twopence,
   I love twopence better than my life;
I spent a penny of it, I lent a penny of it,
   And I took nothing home to my wife.

Oh, my little nothing, jolly little nothing,
   What will nothing buy for my wife?
I have nothing, I spend nothing,
   I love nothing better than my wife.

TWO SIMPLETON SONGS

As I went over the water,
   The water went over me.
I saw two little blackbirds
   Sitting on a tree;
One called me a rascal,
   And one called me a thief,
I took up my little black stick
   And knocked out all their
      teeth.

As I was going along,
   long, long,
A-singing a comical song,
   song, song,
The lane that I went was so
   long, long, long,
And the song that I sung was
   as long, long, long,
And so I went singing along.

SANDY

SANDY he belongs to the mill,
And the mill belongs to Sandy.
Sandy lent a man his mill,
And the man got a loan of Sandy's mill,
And the mill that was lent was Sandy's mill,
And the mill belonged to Sandy.

Bobby Shaftoe

Bobby Shaftoe's gone to
    sea,
Silver buckles at his knee;
He'll come back and marry me,
    Bonny Bobby Shaftoe.

Bobby Shaftoe's bright and fair,
Combing down his yellow hair,
He's my ain for evermair,
    Bonny Bobby Shaftoe.

Bobby Shaftoe's tall and
    slim,
He's always dressed so neat and trim,
The ladies they all keek at him,
    Bonny Bobby Shaftoe.

Bobby Shaftoe's getten a bairn
For to dandle in his arm;
In his arm and on his knee,
    Bobby Shaftoe loves me.

OVER THE WATER TO CHARLIE

Over the water and over the lea,
    And over the water to Charlie.
Charlie loves good ale and wine,
    And Charlie loves good brandy,
And Charlie loves a pretty girl
    As sweet as sugar candy.

Over the water and over the lea,
    And over the water to Charlie.
I'll have none of your nasty beef,
    Nor I'll have none of your barley,
But I'll have some of your very best flour
    To make a white cake for my Charlie.

COCK-A-BANDY

Clap hands, clap hands,
    Hie, Tommy Randy,
Did you see my good man?
    They call him Cock-a-bandy.

Silken stockings on his legs,
    Silver buckles glancin',
A sky-blue bonnet on his head,
    And oh! but he is handsome.

185

THE CARRION CROW

A CARRION crow sat on an oak,
Watching a tailor shape his cloak.
    Sing heigh ho, the carrion crow,
      Fol de riddle, lol de riddle, hi ding do.

The carrion crow began to rave,
And called the tailor a crooked knave.
    Sing heigh ho, the carrion crow,
      Fol de riddle, lol de riddle, hi ding do.

Wife, bring me my old bent bow,
That I may shoot yon carrion crow.
    Sing heigh ho, the carrion crow,
      Fol de riddle, lol de riddle, hi ding do.

The tailor he shot and missed his mark,
And shot his own sow through the heart.
    Sing heigh ho, the carrion crow,
      Fol de riddle, lol de riddle, hi ding do.

Wife, bring brandy in a spoon,
For our old sow is in a swoon.
    Sing heigh ho, the carrion crow,
      Fol de riddle, lol de riddle, hi ding do.

What can the matter be?

O DEAR, what can the matter be?
Dear, dear, what can the matter be?
O dear, what can the matter be?
Johnny's so long at the fair.

He promised he'd buy me a fairing
    should please me,
And then for a kiss, oh! he vowed
    he would tease me,
He promised he'd bring me a bunch of blue ribbons
To tie up my bonny brown hair.

And it's O dear, what can the matter be?
Dear, dear, what can the matter be?
O dear, what can the matter be?
Johnny's so long at the fair.

He promised to buy me a pair of sleeve buttons,
A pair of new garters that cost him but two pence,
He promised he'd bring me a bunch of blue ribbons
To tie up my bonny brown hair.

And it's O dear, what can the matter be?
Dear, dear, what can the matter be?
O dear, what can the matter be?
Johnny's so long at the fair.

He promised he'd bring me a basket of posies,
A garland of lilies, a garland of roses,
A little straw hat, to set off the blue ribbons
That tie up my bonny brown hair.

Three Acres  of Land

My father left me three acres of land,
   Sing ivy, sing ivy;
My father left me three acres of land,
   Sing holly, go whistle and ivy!

I ploughed it with a ram's horn,
   Sing ivy, sing ivy;
And sowed it all over with one peppercorn,
   Sing holly, go whistle and ivy!

I harrowed it with a bramble bush,
   Sing ivy, sing ivy;
And reaped it with my little penknife,
   Sing holly, go whistle and ivy!

I got the mice to carry it to the barn,
   Sing ivy, sing ivy;
And thrashed it with a goose's quill,
   Sing holly, go whistle and ivy!

I got the cat to carry it to the mill,
   Sing ivy, sing ivy;
The miller he swore he would have her paw,
And the cat she swore she would scratch his face,
   Sing holly, go whistle and ivy!

MEDLEY

The cat sat asleep by the side of the fire,
   The mistress snored loud as a pig;
Jack took up his fiddle by Jenny's desire,
   And struck up a bit of a jig.

188

Billy  Boy

WHERE have you been all the day, Billy boy, Billy boy?
Where have you been all the day, my boy Billy?
    I have been all the day
    Courting of a lady gay,
    But oh! she is too young
    To be taken from her mammy.

Is she fit to be thy love, Billy boy, Billy boy?
Is she fit to be thy love, my boy Billy?
    She's as fit to be my love
    As my hand is for my glove,
    But oh! she is too young
    To be taken from her mammy.

Can she brew and can she bake, Billy boy, Billy boy?
Can she brew and can she bake, my boy Billy?
    She can brew and she can bake,
    And she can make a wedding cake,
    But oh! she is too young
    To be taken from her mammy.

Is she fit to be thy wife, Billy boy, Billy boy?
Is she fit to be thy wife, my boy Billy?
    She's as fit to be my wife
    As a sheath is for a knife,
    But oh! she is too young
    To be taken from her mammy.

How old may she be, Billy boy, Billy boy?
How old may she be, my boy Billy?
    Twice six, twice seven,
    Twice twenty and eleven,
    But oh! she is too young
    To be taken from her mammy.

THE FOX'S FORAY

A fox jumped up one winter's night,
And begged the moon to give him light,
For he'd many miles to trot that night
Before he reached his den O!
    Den O! Den O!
For he'd many miles to trot that night
Before he reached his den O!

The first place he came to was a farmer's yard,
Where the ducks and the geese declared it hard
That their nerves should be shaken and their rest so marred
By a visit from Mr. Fox O!
    Fox O! Fox O!
That their nerves should be shaken and their rest so marred
By a visit from Mr. Fox O!

He took the grey goose by the neck,
And swung him right across his back;
The grey goose cried out, Quack, quack, quack,
With his legs hanging dangling down O!
    Down O! Down O!
The grey goose cried out, Quack, quack, quack,
With his legs hanging dangling down O!

Old Mother Slipper Slopper jumped out of bed,
And out of the window she popped her head:
Oh! John, John, John, the grey goose is gone,
And the fox is off to his den O!
    Den O! Den O!
Oh! John, John, John, the grey goose is gone,
And the fox is off to his den O!

John ran up to the top of the hill,
And blew his whistle loud and shrill;
Said the fox, That is very pretty music; still—
I'd rather be in my den O!
    Den O! Den O!
Said the fox, That is very pretty music; still—
I'd rather be in my den O!

The fox went back to his hungry den,
And his dear little foxes, eight, nine, ten;
Quoth they, Good daddy, you must go there again,
If you bring such good cheer from the farm O!
    Farm O! Farm O!
Quoth they, Good daddy, you must go there again,
If you bring such good cheer from the farm O!

The fox and his wife, without any strife,
Said they never ate a better goose in all their life:
They did very well without fork or knife,
And the little ones picked the bones O!
    Bones O! Bones O!
They did very well without fork or knife,
And the little ones picked the bones O!

MY HOBBY HORSE

I HAD a little hobby horse, it was well shod,
It carried me to London, niddety nod,
And when we got to London we heard a great shout,
Down fell my hobby horse and I cried out:
Up again, hobby horse, if thou be a beast,
When we get to our town we will have a feast,
And if there be but little, why thou shalt have some,
And dance to the bag-pipes and beating of the drum.

THE LADY IN LOVE

THERE was a lady loved a swine,
  Honey, quoth she,
Pig-hog wilt thou be mine?
  Hoogh, quoth he.

I'll build thee a silver sty,
  Honey, quoth she,
And in it thou shalt lie.
  Hoogh, quoth he.

Pinned with a silver pin,
  Honey, quoth she,
That thou may go out and in.
  Hoogh, quoth he.

Wilt thou have me now,
  Honey? quoth she.
Speak or my heart will break.
  Hoogh, quoth he.

THE LAST WILL AND TESTAMENT
OF THE GREY MARE

JOHN Cook had a little grey mare,
  He, haw, hum!
Her back stood up and her bones were bare,
  He, haw, hum!

John Cook was riding up Shooter's Bank,
  He, haw, hum!
And there his nag did kick and prank,
  He, haw, hum!

John Cook was riding up Shooter's Hill,
  He, haw, hum!
His mare fell down and she made her will,
  He, haw, hum!

The bridle and saddle he laid on the shelf,
  He, haw, hum!
If you want any more you may sing it yourself,
  He, haw, hum!

Ten Little Injuns

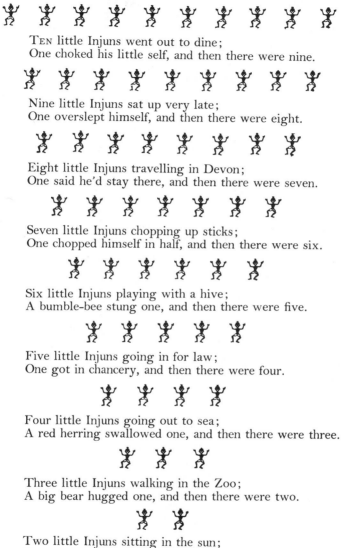

TEN little Injuns went out to dine;
One choked his little self, and then there were nine.

Nine little Injuns sat up very late;
One overslept himself, and then there were eight.

Eight little Injuns travelling in Devon;
One said he'd stay there, and then there were seven.

Seven little Injuns chopping up sticks;
One chopped himself in half, and then there were six.

Six little Injuns playing with a hive;
A bumble-bee stung one, and then there were five.

Five little Injuns going in for law;
One got in chancery, and then there were four.

Four little Injuns going out to sea;
A red herring swallowed one, and then there were three.

Three little Injuns walking in the Zoo;
A big bear hugged one, and then there were two.

Two little Injuns sitting in the sun;
One got frizzled up, and then there was one.

One little Injun living all alone;
He got married, and then there were none.

The Comedy of  Billy and Betty

When shall we be married,
  Billy, my own sweet lad?
We shall be married tomorrow,
  If you think it is good.
Shall we be married no sooner,
  Billy, my own sweet lad?
Would you be married tonight?
  I think that the girl is gone mad.

Who shall we ask to the wedding,
  Billy, my own sweet lad?
We shall ask father and mother,
  If you think it is good.
Shall we ask nobody else,
  Billy, my own sweet lad?
Would you ask King and Queen?
  I think that the girl is gone mad.

What shall we have for the dinner,
  Billy, my own sweet lad?
We shall have bacon and beans,
  If you think it is good.
Shall we have nothing more,
  Billy, my own sweet lad?
Would you have peaches and cream?
  I think that the girl is gone mad.

What shall I wear to the wedding,
  Billy, my own sweet lad?
You have your apron and gown,
  If you think it is good.
Shall I wear nothing that's finer,
  Billy, my own sweet lad?
Would you wear satin and silk?
  I think that the girl is gone mad.

How shall I go to the church,
  Billy, my own sweet lad?
You shall ride in my wheelbarrow,
  If you think it is good.
Shall I have nothing that's better,
  Billy, my own sweet lad?
Would you have horses and coach?
  I think that the girl is gone mad.

Merrily danced the Quaker's Wife

THE Quaker's wife got up to bake,
 Her children all about her;
She gave them every one a cake,
 And there the miller found her.

He chased her up, he chased her
  down,
 As fast as he could make her;
And merrily danced the Quaker's
  wife,
 And merrily danced the Quaker.

Sugar and spice and all things nice,
 And all things very good in it;
And then the miller sat down to play
 A tune upon the spinet.

Chorus

Merrily danced the Quaker's wife,
 And merrily danced the Quaker,
Merrily, merrily, merrily, merrily,
 Merrily danced the Quaker.

CAROUSAL

WE'RE all dry with drinking on't,
We're all dry with drinking on't,
The piper kissed the fiddler's wife,
And I can't sleep for thinking on't.

COURTSHIP

I LOVE thee, Betty,
 Do'st thou, Johnny?
Hey, but I wonder where!
 In my heart, Betty.
 In thy heart, Johnny?
Thou never yet made it appear.

But I'll wed thee, Betty.
 Wed me, Johnny?
Hey, but I wonder when!
 On Sunday, Betty.
 On Sunday, Johnny?
Hey, I wish it was Sunday then.

195

THE LOVER'S
TASKS

Can you make me a cambric shirt,
 Parsley, sage, rosemary, and thyme,
Without any seam or needlework?
 And you shall be a true lover of mine.

Can you wash it in yonder well,
 Parsley, sage, rosemary, and thyme,
Where never sprung water, nor rain ever fell?
 And you shall be a true lover of mine.

Can you dry it on yonder thorn,
 Parsley, sage, rosemary, and thyme,
Which never bore blossom since Adam was born?
 And you shall be a true lover of mine.

Now you've asked me questions three,
 Parsley, sage, rosemary, and thyme,
I hope you'll answer as many for me,
 And you shall be a true lover of mine.

Can you find me an acre of land,
 Parsley, sage, rosemary, and thyme,
Between the salt water and the sea sand?
 And you shall be a true lover of mine.

Can you plough it with a ram's horn,
 Parsley, sage, rosemary, and thyme,
And sow it all over with one peppercorn?
 And you shall be a true lover of mine.

Can you reap it with a sickle of leather,
  Parsley, sage, rosemary, and thyme,
And bind it up with a peacock's feather?
  And you shall be a true lover of mine.

When you have done and finished your work,
  Parsley, sage, rosemary, and thyme,
Then come to me for your cambric shirt,
  And you shall be a true lover of mine.

THE LOVER'S GIFTS

My love sent me a chicken without e'er a bone;
He sent me a cherry without e'er a stone;
He sent me a Bible that no man could read;
He sent me a blanket without e'er a thread.

How can there be a chicken without e'er a bone?
How can there be a cherry without e'er a stone?
How can there be a Bible that no man can read?
How can there be a blanket without e'er a thread?

When the chicken's in the eggshell, there is no bone;
When the cherry's in the blossom, there is no stone;
When the Bible's in the press, no man can it read;
When the wool is on the sheep's back, there is no thread.

THE TWELVE DAYS OF CHRISTMAS

THE first day of Christmas
My true love sent to me
A partridge in a pear tree.

The second day of Christmas
My true love sent to me
Two turtle doves, and
A partridge in a pear tree.

The third day of Christmas
My true love sent to me
Three French hens,   •
Two turtle doves, and
A partridge in a pear tree.

The fourth day of Christmas
My true love sent to me
Four colly birds,
Three French hens,
Two turtle doves, and
A partridge in a pear tree.

The fifth day of Christmas
My true love sent to me
Five gold rings,

Four colly birds,
Three French hens,
Two turtle doves, and
A partridge in a pear tree.

The sixth day of Christmas
My true love sent to me
Six geese a-laying,
Five gold rings,
Four colly birds,
Three French hens,
Two turtle doves, and
A partridge in a pear tree.

The seventh day of Christmas
My true love sent to me
Seven swans a-swimming,
Six geese a-laying,
Five gold rings,
Four colly birds,
Three French hens,
Two turtle doves, and
A partridge in a pear tree.

The eighth day of Christmas
My true love sent to me
Eight maids a-milking,

Seven swans a-swimming,
Six geese a-laying,
Five gold rings,
Four colly birds,
Three French hens,
Two turtle doves, and
A partridge in a pear tree.

The ninth day of Christmas
My true love sent to me
Nine drummers drumming,
Eight maids a-milking,
Seven swans a-swimming,
Six geese a-laying,
Five gold rings,
Four colly birds,
Three French hens,
Two turtle doves, and
A partridge in a pear tree.

The tenth day of Christmas
My true love sent to me
Ten pipers piping,
Nine drummers drumming,
Eight maids a-milking,
Seven swans a-swimming,
Six geese a-laying,
Five gold rings,
Four colly birds,
Three French hens,

Two turtle doves, and
A partridge in a pear tree.

The eleventh day of Christmas
My true love sent to me
Eleven ladies dancing,
Ten pipers piping,
Nine drummers drumming,
Eight maids a-milking,
Seven swans a-swimming,
Six geese a-laying,
Five gold rings,
Four colly birds,
Three French hens,
Two turtle doves, and
A partridge in a pear tree.

The twelfth day of Christmas
My true love sent to me
Twelve lords a-leaping,
Eleven ladies dancing,
Ten pipers piping,
Nine drummers drumming,
Eight maids a-milking,
Seven swans a-swimming,
Six geese a-laying,
Five gold rings,
Four colly birds,
Three French hens,
Two turtle doves, and
A partridge in a pear tree.

A SHIP A-SAILING

I saw a ship a-sailing,
　A-sailing on the sea,
And oh, but it was laden
　With pretty things for thee!

There were comfits in the cabin,
　And apples in the hold;
The sails were made of silk,
　And the masts were all of
　　gold.

The four-and-twenty sailors,
　That stood between the decks,
Were four-and-twenty white
　mice
　With chains about their necks.

The captain was a duck
　With a packet on his back,
And when the ship began to
　move
　The captain said, Quack!
　Quack!

Dame, get up and bake your pies,
　Bake your pies, bake your pies;
Dame, get up and bake your pies,
　On Christmas day in the morning.

Dame, what makes your maidens lie,
　Maidens lie, maidens lie;
Dame, what makes your maidens lie,
　On Christmas day in the morning?

Dame, what makes your ducks to die,
　Ducks to die, ducks to die;
Dame, what makes your ducks to die,
　On Christmas day in the morning?

Their wings are cut and they cannot fly,
　Cannot fly, cannot fly;
Their wings are cut and they cannot fly,
　On Christmas day in the morning.

KING ARTHUR

When good King Arthur ruled this land,
　He was a goodly King;
He stole three pecks of barley-meal
　To make a bag-pudding.

A bag-pudding the King did make,
　And stuffed it well with plums,
And in it put great lumps of fat,
　As big as my two thumbs.

The King and Queen did eat thereof,
　And noblemen beside;
And what they could not eat that night,
　The Queen next morning fried.

WHY MAY NOT I LOVE JOHNNY?

JOHNNY shall have a new bonnet,
  And Johnny shall go to the fair,
And Johnny shall have a blue ribbon
  To tie up his bonny brown hair.

And why may not I love Johnny?
  And why may not Johnny love me?
And why may not I love Johnny
  As well as another body?

And here's a leg for a stocking,
  And here's a leg for a shoe,
And he has a kiss for his daddy,
  And two for his mammy, I trow.

And why may not I love Johnny?
  And why may not Johnny love me?
And why may not I love Johnny
  As well as another body?

A LITTLE cock sparrow sat on a green
  tree,
And he chirruped, he chirruped, so merry
  was he.
A naughty boy came with his wee bow
  and arrow,
Says he, I will shoot this little cock
  sparrow.
His body will make me a nice little stew,
And his giblets will make me a little pie
  too.
Oh, no, said the sparrow, I won't make
  a stew,
So he clapped his wings and away he flew.

INDUCEMENTS

WHISTLE, daughter, whistle,
  And you shall have a sheep.
Mother, I cannot whistle,
  Neither can I sleep.

Whistle, daughter, whistle,
  And you shall have a cow.
Mother, I cannot whistle,
  Neither know I how.

Whistle, daughter, whistle,
  And you shall have a man.
Mother, I cannot whistle,
  But I'll do the best I can.

BESSY AND MARY

BESSY Bell and Mary Gray,
  They were two bonnie lasses;
They built their house upon the
  lea,
And covered it with rushes.

Bessy kept the garden gate,
  And Mary kept the pantry;
Bessy always had to wait,
  While Mary lived in plenty.

Tommy  O'Linn

TOMMY O'Linn was a Scotsman born,
His head was bald and his beard was shorn:
He had a cap made of a hare's skin,
An alderman was Tommy O'Linn.

Tommy O'Linn had no boots to put on,
But two calves' skins with the hair all gone:
They were split at the side, and the water went in,
It's damp to the feet, said Tommy O'Linn.

Tommy O'Linn had no coat to put on,
He borrowed a goatskin to make himself one:
He planted the horns right under his chin,
They'll answer for pistols, said Tommy O'Linn.

Tommy O'Linn had no breeches to wear,
So he got him a sheepskin to make him a pair,
With the skinny side out and the woolly side in,
Aha! this is warm, said Tommy O'Linn.

Tommy O'Linn had no watch to put on,
So he scooped out a turnip to make himself one:
He caught a cricket, and put it within,
It is my own ticker, said Tommy O'Linn.

Tommy O'Linn went to bring his wife home,
He had but one horse that was all skin and bone:
I'll put her behind me as neat as a pin,
And her mother before me, said Tommy O'Linn.

Tommy O'Linn, his wife and wife's mother,
They all went over the bridge together:
The bridge broke down and they all tumbled in,
We'll find ground at the bottom, said Tommy O'Linn.

The Croodin Doo

WHERE hae ye been a' the day,
My bonny wee croodin doo?
O I hae been at my stepmother's
    house;
Make my bed, mammie, now, now,
    now!
Make my bed, mammie, now!

Where did ye get your dinner,
My bonny wee croodin doo?
I got it in my stepmother's;
Make my bed, mammie, now, now,
    now!
Make my bed, mammie, now!

What did she gie ye to your dinner,
My bonny wee croodin doo?
She ga'e me a little four-footed fish;
Make my bed, mammie, now, now,
    now!
Make my bed, mammie, now!

Where got she the four-footed fish,
My bonny wee croodin doo?
She got it down in yon well strand;
O make my bed, mammie, now, now,
    now!
Make my bed, mammie, now!

What did she do wi' the banes o't,
My bonny wee croodin doo?
She ga'e them to the little dog;
Make my bed, mammie, now, now,
    now!
Make my bed, mammie, now!

O what became o' the little dog,
My bonny wee croodin doo?
O it shot out its feet and died!
O make my bed mammie, now, now,
    now!
Make my bed, mammie, now!

THE SQUIRREL

THE winds they did blow,
    The leaves they did wag;
Along came a beggar boy,
    And put me in his bag.

He took me up to London,
    A lady did me buy,
Put me in a silver cage,
    And hung me up on high.

With apples by the fire,
    And nuts for to crack,
Besides a little feather bed
    To rest my little back.

Three Ships

I saw three ships come sailing by,
  Come sailing by, come sailing by,
I saw three ships come sailing by,
  On New-Year's day in the morning.

And what do you think was in them then,
  Was in them then, was in them then?
And what do you think was in them then,
  On New-Year's day in the morning?

Three pretty girls were in them then,
  Were in them then, were in them then,
Three pretty girls were in them then,
  On New-Year's day in the morning.

One could whistle, and one could sing,
  And one could play on the violin;
Such joy there was at my wedding,
  On New-Year's day in the morning.

CAROL

As I sat on a sunny bank
On Christmas day in the morning,
I saw three ships come sailing by
On Christmas day in the morning.
And who do you think were in those ships
But Joseph and his fair lady;
He did whistle and she did sing,
And all the bells on earth did ring
For joy our Saviour he was born
On Christmas day in the morning.

The Derby Ram

As I was going to Derby
  Upon a market day,
I met the finest ram, sir,
  That ever was fed on hay.

This ram was fat behind, sir,
  This ram was fat before,
This ram was three yards high, sir,
  Indeed he was no more.

The wool upon his back, sir,
  Reached up unto the sky,
The eagles built their nests there,
  For I heard the young ones cry.

The wool upon his tail, sir,
  Was three yards and an ell,
Of it they made a rope, sir,
  To pull the parish bell.

The space between the horns, sir,
  Was as far as man could reach,
And there they built a pulpit,
  But no one in it preached.

This ram had four legs to walk upon,
  This ram had four legs to stand,
And every leg he had, sir,
  Stood on an acre of land.

Now the man that fed the ram, sir,
  He fed him twice a day,
And each time that he fed him, sir,
  He ate a rick of hay.

The man that killed the ram, sir,
  Was up to his knees in blood,
And the boy that held the pail, sir,
  Was carried away in the flood.

Indeed, sir, it's the truth, sir,
  For I never was taught to lie,
And if you go to Derby, sir,
  You may eat a bit of the pie.

Three Brethren from Spain

WE are three brethren out of Spain,
Come to court your daughter Jane.

My daughter Jane she is too young,
She has no skill in the flattering tongue.

Be she young, or be she old,
It's for her gold she must be sold;
So fare thee well, my lady gay,
I must turn another way.

Turn back, turn back, thou Spanish knight,
And rub your spurs till they be bright.

My spurs are bright and richly wrought,
And in this town they were not bought;
Nor in this town will they be sold,
Neither for silver nor for gold.
So fare thee well, my lady gay,
For I must turn another way.

Turn back, turn back, thou scornful knight,
And take the fairest in thy sight.

The fairest maid that I can see
Is pretty Nancy—come to me.

Here comes my daughter safe and sound,
Every pocket with a thousand pound;
Every finger with a gay gold ring;
Please to take my daughter in.

The Old Woman who bought a Pig

AN old woman went to market and bought a pig;
Pig had four legs,
But pig would not go.
Well, says the old woman, what shall I do?

She went a little farther and she calls to a dog,
Dog, dog, bite pig,
Pig will not go,
And I should have been at home two hours ago.
But the dog would not.

She went a little farther and she calls to a stick,
Stick, stick, beat dog,
Dog won't bite pig,
Pig will not go,
And I should have been at home two hours ago.
But the stick would not.

She went a little farther and she calls to a fire,
Fire, fire, burn stick,
Stick won't beat dog,
Dog won't bite pig,
Pig will not go,
And I should have been at home two hours ago.
But the fire would not.

She went a little farther and she calls to some
    water,
Water, water, quench fire,
Fire won't burn stick,
Stick won't beat dog,
Dog won't bite pig,
Pig will not go,
And I should have been at home two hours ago.
But the water would not.

She went a little farther and she calls to an ox,
Ox, ox, drink water,
Water won't quench fire,
Fire won't burn stick,
Stick won't beat dog,
Dog won't bite pig,
Pig will not go,
And I should have been at home two hours ago.
    But the ox would not.

She went a little farther and she calls to a butcher,
Butcher, butcher, kill ox,
Ox won't drink water,
Water won't quench fire,
Fire won't burn stick,
Stick won't beat dog,
Dog won't bite pig,
Pig will not go,
And I should have been at home two hours ago.
    But the butcher would not.

She went a little farther and she calls to a rope,
Rope, rope, hang butcher,
Butcher won't kill ox,
Ox won't drink water,
Water won't quench fire,
Fire won't burn stick,
Stick won't beat dog,
Dog won't bite pig,
Pig will not go,
And I should have been at home two hours ago.
    But the rope would not.

She went a little farther and she calls to a rat,
Rat, rat, gnaw rope,
Rope won't hang butcher,
Butcher won't kill ox,
Ox won't drink water,
Water won't quench fire,
Fire won't burn stick,
Stick won't beat dog,
Dog won't bite pig,
Pig will not go,
And I should have been at home two hours ago.
  But the rat would not.

She went a little farther and she calls to a cat,
Cat, cat, kill rat,
Rat won't gnaw rope,
Rope won't hang butcher,
Butcher won't kill ox,
Ox won't drink water,
Water won't quench fire,
Fire won't burn stick,
Stick won't beat dog,
Dog won't bite pig,
Pig will not go,
And I should have been at home two hours ago.

Then the cat began to kill the rat,
The rat began to gnaw the rope,
The rope began to hang the butcher,
The butcher began to kill the ox,
The ox began to drink the water,
The water began to quench the fire,
The fire began to burn the stick,
The stick began to beat the dog,
The dog began to bite the pig,
The pig began to go;
  So it's all over, and the old woman's home again now.

OUR bow's bended,
Our book's ended,
If you do not like a bit
You may mend it.

Sources of the Illustrations

MOST of the illustrations come from toy books and chapbooks of the latter part of the eighteenth century, and the first half of the nineteenth century. The earliest known nursery rhyme book *Tommy Thumb's (Pretty) Song Book* was published 'for the Diversion of all Little Masters and Misses' in 1744, and was issued in two volumes, price sixpence a volume, bound and gilt. Like many of its successors in the next eighty years it was of midget proportions, with pages $3 \times 1\frac{3}{4}$ inches, each page containing a single rhyme usually headed by a miniature engraving. This layout was adopted at the beginning of the nineteenth century for the little nursery rhyme chapbooks which were sold up and down the country, in market places and at cottage doors, for a penny or a halfpenny. Being designed to be carried by hawkers or 'petty chapmen', the chapbooks seldom had stiff covers which would add unnecessary weight to the pedlar's pack, and sometimes they consisted simply of a single sheet folded over three times to make sixteen pages. Chapbook printers were rarely original in what they printed, and although their presses were widely separated in different parts of the country their productions closely resembled each other. The woodcuts they employed were often old blocks retouched, or copied, or bought from each other, the same blocks sometimes doing service in one publication after another, and a number of the illustrations we have reproduced can be found in publications other than the sources we cite, while some of the illustrations undoubtedly first appeared in earlier editions than now survive.

To indicate the precise illustration referred to in each entry, the number of the page on which it appears is succeeded, where there is more than one illustration on the page, by a small identifying letter. These letters, beginning with *a* on each page, have been given to the illustrations from the top of the page downwards, the left being lettered before the right where illustrations are on the same level, for example:

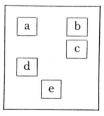

1744 *Tommy Thumb's (Pretty) Song Book*, vol. ii (London: M. Cooper), 86d, 87d e, 91d, 142c, 143a, 195b.

c. 1758 *Food for the Mind: or, A New Riddle-Book* (London: J. Newbery), 148c, 149b d f, 152a. From 1787 edition.

SOURCES OF THE ILLUSTRATIONS

1776 *Juvenile Sports and Pastimes* (London: T. Carnan), 201b.

1780 *Mother Goose's Melody* (London: T. Carnan), 6a b, 10a, 18, 82c, 138b, 177, 206. From *c.* 1795 edition.

1783 *A Curious Hieroglyphick Bible* (London: T. Hodgson), 167 top line of birds. From 1796 edition.

1787 *A Little Pretty Pocket-Book* (Worcester, Massachusetts: Isaiah Thomas), 115a.

1788 *Tommy Thumb's Song Book* (Worcester, Massachusetts: Isaiah Thomas), 23e, 40c.

1792 *The Looking-Glass for the Mind* (London: E. Newbery), 'Cuts designed and engraved on wood by [John] Bewick', 116, 117, 127a, 175.

1795 *Robin Hood* (London: J. Johnson), engravings by John Bewick, 126a b (detail).

1797 *History of British Birds*, vol. i, 'The Figures engraved on Wood by T. Bewick', 67a, 129.

1798 Mrs. M. S. Pilkington, *Historical Beauties for Young Ladies*, 31c, 174.

c. 1800 *Vocal Harmony, or No Song, No Supper* (no imprint), 23b, 26a d, 27c, 71a b c, 94c, 95a. See also Johnson's *Nursery Rhymes, c.* 1830.

1805 *The Cries of London* (London: J. Harris), 73b c.

1806 Sol. Hodgson, *The Hive of Ancient and Modern Literature*, engravings reproduced are probably by Luke Clennell, 60c, 130a b, 131a b, 191.

1808 *Poetical Works of Robert Burns* (Alnwick: Catnach and Davison), 'engravings on wood by Mr. [T.] Bewick, from original designs by Mr. Thurston', 66b, 181.

1808 *The Cries of London* (London: J. T. Ward & Co.), 72a.

c. 1808 *The Lottery* (London: J. T. Ward & Co.), 127b.

1809 *A History of British Birds*. 'The Figures Engraved on Wood by T. Bewick', 194b.

c. 1810 *Jerry Diddle and his Fiddle* (no imprint), 127c, 142c.
[Cover missing] Douce Adds. 6 (12), 96c.
[Cover missing] Douce Adds. 34 (3), 60b.
Woodblock engraved by James Lee, 66a.

1814 *Tom Thumb's Play-Book* (Edinburgh: G. Ross), 60a.

1815 *Tommy Thumb's Song-Book* (Glasgow: J. Lumsden & Son), 3, 178a.

c. 1815 *Sir Gregory Guess's Present to Master Robin Readywit* (London: T. Batchelar), 148f.
The Picture Book (Otley: William Walker), 86c, 176, 194a.
The Diverting History of Old Mother Hubbard and her Dog (Otley: William Walker), 29d, 30b d e.

1818 *The Fables of Æsop, and Others*, 'With Designs on Wood, by Thomas Bewick', 52a, 153e, 172, 195a.

1820 *Select Fables*, 'With Cuts, Designed and Engraved by Thomas and John Bewick and Others, previous to the year 1784', 26b, 105a, 128, 190.

c. 1820 *Jack Horner's Pretty Toy* (London: J. E. Evans), 207b c d e, 208a b c, 209a b c.

SOURCES OF THE ILLUSTRATIONS

c. 1820 *Jumping Joan* (London: J. E. Evans), 23c d, 52c e, 53c d, 148d.

Old Mother Goose; or, The Golden Egg (London: J. E. Evans), 6c, 85d, 88a b c d e f, 89a b c d e f, 90a b c, 139c.

The History of Little King Pippin (Wellington, Salop: F. Houlston and Son), 83c.

Nurse Dandlem's Little Repository (Wellington, Salop: F. Houlston and Son), 58b.

The Cheerful Warbler (York: J. Kendrew), 58d, 91a c.

The Courtship of Cock Robin and Jenny Wren (York: J. Kendrew), 168d.

An Elegy on the Death and Burial of Cock Robin (York: J. Kendrew), 166a b c d e, 167b c d e f, 168a b c.

The Foundling (York: J. Kendrew), 100d.

The History of a Little Boy Found Under an Haycock (York: James Kendrew), 101c.

The History of Little Tom Tucker (York: J. Kendrew), 59d, 98d, 123b.

The History of Sam, the Sportsman (York: J. Kendrew), 44b.

The History of Simple Simon (York: J. Kendrew), 43a b c d e.

The House that Jack Built (York: J. Kendrew), 47a b d e, 48a b c, 49a.

Jack and Jill, and Old Dame Gill (York: J. Kendrew), 42a b c d e.

The Life and Death of Jenny Wren (York: J. Kendrew), 41d.

The Life of Jack Sprat (York: J. Kendrew), 44d, 45d, 52f, 90d e, 100b, 101b.

Old Dame Trot, and Her Comical Cat (York: J. Kendrew), 53e, 100c.

The Silver Penny (York: J. Kendrew), 97b.

Tom, the Piper's Son (York: J. Kendrew), 46a b c d.

The World Turned Upside Down (York: J. Kendrew), 143b.

The History of Dick Whittington (Banbury: J. G. Rusher), 200a.

The New House that Jack Built (Banbury: J. G. Rusher), 47c.

Poetic Trifles, or Pretty Poems for Young Folks (Banbury: J. G. Rusher), 84d.

The Riddler's Riddle Book (Banbury: J. G. Rusher), 148b.

1821 *A Supplement to the History of British Birds*, 'The Figures engraved on Wood by T. Bewick', 125b.

1822 *The Story Teller* (London: J. Harris and Son), 96a, 97a.

1824 T. Clark, *The English Mother's Catechism for her Children*, 32b, 53b, 58c, 59a, 72c, 75b c, 139a, 152b.

1824 *Æsop's Fables* (Dublin: W. Espy), 74e.

c. 1825 Robert Huish, *Edwin and Henry*, 'Designs by Brook engraved by Robert Branston', 187b.

The Temple of Fancy (London: Whittingham and Arliss), engravings by Robert Branston, 135, 152d, 153b.

Jerry Diddle, and his Fiddle (London: J. Catnach), 98c.

Nurse Love-Child's Legacy (London: J. Catnach), 143c.

The Babes in the Wood (Alnwick: W. Davison), 99b.

Tom Thumb's Play Book (Alnwick: W. Davison), 207a.

The Three Silver Trouts (Derby: H. Mozley), 27b.

A Collection of Nursery Rhymes (Edinburgh: Oliver & Boyd), 41e, 45b, 91b.

SOURCES OF THE ILLUSTRATIONS

c. 1825   *The History of Peter Martin* (Edinburgh: Oliver & Boyd), 86e.
          The Poetical Alphabet (Edinburgh: Oliver & Boyd), 69a b c d.
          Tom Thumb's Play-Book (Edinburgh: Oliver & Boyd), 84c.
          Jacky Dandy's Delight (Leeds: J. Roberts), 99c.
          The Little Woman and the Pedlar (Leeds: Joseph Roberts), 169a b c.

     1827   *Vignettes*, engraved by Thomas Bewick, 67b, 95b, 112, 180.

     1828   Ingram Cobbin, *Elements of English Grammar*, 'With cuts by [Robert]
          Branston', 31b, 32c d, 33a b, 77b, 94d, 189.

c. 1830   *The Good Child's Ménage* (London: S. Carvalho), 149e.
          The Good Little Mouse (London: Dean and Munday), 7b, 31a, 52g.
          Nursery Rhymes (London: W. S. Johnson), 23a, 26c, 27a, 70a, 94a,
          95c. These cuts also appear in *Vocal Harmony*, *c.* 1800.
          Cradle Melodies (Derby: Thomas Richardson), 44c.
          Richardson's New Battledore (Derby: Thomas Richardson), 17b.
          Richardson's New Royal Battledore (Derby: Thomas Richardson), 105b.

     1831   *The Nursery and Infants' School Magazine*, edited by Mrs. Lucy Cam-
          eron, 75d, 82e, 85e, 114b.

     1832   Mrs. L. M. Child, *The Girl's Own Book*, 'Wood cuts engraved by
          Branston and Wright', 32d, 77a.

c. 1833   *Mother Goose's Melodies* (Boston, Massachusetts: Munroe and Francis),
          45a.
          Peter Parley, *Tales of Animals*, engravings after designs by William
          Harvey, 53a, 60d, 95d.

c. 1834   *The History of Puss in Boots* (Derby: Thomas Richardson), 83a.
          The House that Jack Built (Derby: Thomas Richardson), woodcuts prob-
          ably by Orlando Jewitt, 83d.
          A Natural History of Beasts and Birds (Derby: T. Richardson), woodcut
          probably by Orlando Jewitt, 114a.
          The Picture Alphabet (Derby: Thomas Richardson), woodcuts probably
          by Orlando Jewitt, 106 all, 107 all except 'R'.
          Richardson's Child's Instructer [*sic*] (Derby: Thomas Richardson), 11, 49b.

c. 1835   *William Walker and his Pony Bob* (Birmingham: T. Brandred), 33c.
          The Amusing History of Mother Goose (Devonport: S. & J. Keys), v,
          86a, 201a.
          The Bee-Hive (Devonport: Samuel and John Keys), 122a b, 123a, 149c.
          The Child's Gift (Devonport: S. & J. Keys), 17c.
          Cradle Melodies (Devonport: S. & J. Keys), 40b, 45c, 85a, 87b.
          The History of Jacky Jingle (Devonport: S. & J. Keys), 84b.
          The House that Jack Built (Devonport: Samuel and John Keys), 48d.
          The Present (Devonport: S. & J. Keys), 96b.
          Puzzlecap's Amusing Riddle Book (Devonport: S. & J. Keys), 61c, 153f.
          The Serio-Comic Drama of Punch and Judy (Devonport: Samuel and
          John Keys), 98a.
          Tom, The Piper's Son (Devonport: Samuel and John Keys), 164a b c,
          165a b c d.
          The Happy Girl (London: Religious Tract Society), 10b.

c. 1840   *The Illustrated A. B. C.* (Sudbury: H. M. Ives), 59c.
          The Puzzle-Cap (Derby: Henry Mozley and Son), 33e.

SOURCES OF THE ILLUSTRATIONS

c. 1840 *Nursery Rhymes* (London: Richardson and Son), 41a b, 44a, 84a, 85b, 99a, 140, 186.

The Riddle Book (London: Richardson and Son), woodcuts probably by Orlando Jewitt, 33f, 82b, 85e, 148e, 153d, 204.

Death and Burial of Cock Robin (Banbury: J. G. Rusher), 74c, 149a.

Life and Adventures of Robinson Crusoe (Banbury: J. G. Rusher), 82d.

The Life of Jack Sprat (Banbury: J. G. Rusher), 188.

Nursery Rhymes, from the Royal Collections (Banbury: J. G. Rusher), 59b.

Old Mother Hubbard and Her Dog (Banbury: J. G. Rusher), 28a d, 29a b c e, 30a.

Poetic Trifles, for Young Gentlemen and Ladies (Banbury: J. G. Rusher), 76, 205.

The Renowned History of Dame Trot and Her Cat (Banbury: J. G. Rusher), 94b.

The Amusing Riddle-Book (Montrose: James Watt), 31d, 87c, 97d, 148a, 152c e, 200b.

c. 1843 *The Cries of Banbury and London* (Banbury: J. G. Rusher), 72b d, 73a.

c. 1845 *The Royal Nursery Spelling and Reading Book* (London: Dean & Son), 115b.

A was an Archer (Derby: Henry Mozley and Sons), 100a.

Puss in Boots (Derby: Henry Mozley and Sons), 83b.

Old Dan Tucker (Durham: Walker), song sheet heading, 63b.

Nursery Rhymes (London: Webb, Millington and Co.), 98b.

1850 *A Picture Story Book* (London: Geo. Routledge and Co.), 101a.

c. 1850 *Cradle Rhymes for Infants* (Derby: John and Charles Mozley), 41c, 82a.

Walker's Specimens of Wood Engravings (Durham: Walker), 40a d, 142a, 187a.

Book of Games and Amusements (London: W. Tegg & Co.), 124, 141.

1851 *Songs for the Nursery* (London: Darton & Co.), 32a.

---

c. 1860 *The History of an Apple Pie* (London: William S. Fortey), 108 all, 109 all except 'U', 138c.

Nineteenth-century printers' ornaments, 52b d, 113e f g, 177b.

1862 *Routledge's Nursery Picture Book*, 96d.

1865 *Impressions from Wood Blocks*, 'Engraved by Bewick and others', 113c d, 203.

1870 T. Hugo, *Bewick's Woodcuts*, not all attributable to Bewick, 7a, 86b, 87a, 183d, 202.

1885 *Thomas Bewick's Works*, vol. i, 75a.

1886 Julia Boyd, *Bewick Gleanings*, 154.

c. 1887 A. W. Tuer, 1000 *Quaint Cuts*, 97c.

1890 Edwin Pearson, *Banbury Chap Books and Nursery Toy Book Literature*, 61a, 113a b, 139b.

In line with the chapbook tradition some of the illustrations have been retouched so that they could be reproduced in the present work, and a few have been reduced. All illustrations not listed are by Joan Hassall.

Index of First Lines, Refrains, and Familiar Titles

Note: Titles of rhymes are in italics, and are not preceded by the definite or indefinite article.

INDEX OF FIRST LINES

INDEX OF FIRST LINES

INDEX OF FIRST LINES

INDEX OF FIRST LINES

Lavender's blue, diddle, diddle, 181.
Lazy deuks that sit i' the coal-neuks, 58.
Leg over leg, 14.
Let's go to the wood, says this pig, 5.
Lilies are white, 60.
Little Betty Blue, 87.
Little Betty Pringle she had a pig, 36.
Little Billy Breek, 147.
Little bird of paradise, 153.
Little Blue Ben, who lives in the glen, 101.
Little Blue Betty lived in a den, 97.
Little Bob Robin, 50.
Little Bo-peep has lost her sheep, 64.
Little Boy Blue, 38.
Little Dicky Dilver, 102.
Little fishes in a brook, 25.
Little General Monk, 41.
Little girl, little girl, 99.
Little Jack Dandy-prat, 123.
Little Jack Horner, 45; *see also* 54.
Little Jack Sprat, 45.
Little John Jiggy Jag, 83.
Little Johnny Morgan, 91.
Little King Pippin he built a fine hall, 85.
Little lad, little lad, 121.
Little maid, pretty maid, 124.
Little Man and the Little Maid, 176–7.
Little man in coal pit, 16.
Little Miss Muffet, 39.
Little Moppet, 96.
Little Nancy Etticoat, 153.
Little Pig, 5.
Little Poll Parrot, 52.
Little Polly Flinders, 37.
Little pretty Nancy girl, 122.
Little Robin Redbreast came to visit me, 51.
Little Robin Redbreast sat upon a rail, 51.
Little Robin Redbreast sat upon a tree, 51.
Little Tee-Wee, 32.
Little Tom Tittlemouse, 27.
Little Tommy Tacket, 99.
Little Tommy Tittlemouse, 27.
Little Tommy Tucker, 44.
Little Woman and the Pedlar, 169.
Lock the dairy door, 53.
London Bridge is broken down, 76.
Long legs, crooked thighs, 149.
Love-Sick Frog, 172–4.
Lucy Locket lost her pocket, 70.
Lumpety, lumpety, lump, *see* 13.

Mackerel sky, 117.
Magpie, magpie, flutter and flee, 74.
Make my bed, mammie, now, now, now, *see* 203.
Make three-fourths of a cross, 155.
Manners in the dining-room, 115.
March, march, head erect, 77.
March winds and April showers, 118.
Margery Mutton-pie, 123.
Mary had a little lamb, 36.

Mary, Mary, quite contrary, 27.
Master I have, and I am his man, 96.
Matthew, Mark, Luke, and John, 17, 77.
Merrily danced the Quaker's wife, *see* 195.
Milk-Maid, 175.
Millery, millery, dustipole, 74.
Miss Muffet, 39.
Miss One, Two, and Three, 93.
Mocking Bird, see 18.
Moll-in-the-wad and I fell out, 31.
Monday's child is fair of face, xiv.
Moon, moon, 17.
Moses supposes his toeses are roses, 156.
Mother Goose, 88–90.
Mother Hubbard, 28–30.
Mother, may I go out to swim? 144.
Mother Niddity Nod, 94.
Mother Shuttle, 81.
Mr. East gave a feast, 92.
Mr. Ibister, and Betsy his sister, 101.
Mrs. Mason bought a basin, 93.
My bonnie wee croodin doo, *see* 203.
My dame hath a lame tame crane, 156.
My fair lady, *see* 76.
My father died a month ago, 63.
My father he died, but I can't tell you how, 180.
My father left me three acres of land, 188.
My father was a Frenchman, 9.
My grandmother sent me, 156.
My little old man and I fell out, 31.
My love sent me a chicken without e'er a bone, 197.
My maid Mary, 58.
My mammy's maid, 96.
My mill grinds pepper and spice, 143.
My mother and your mother, 78.
My mother said, 127.
My true love sent to me, *see* 198–9.

Nancy Cock, 83.
Nauty Pauty Jack-a-Dandy, 23.
Needles and pins, needles and pins, *see* 116.
Nievie nievie nick nack, 9.
Nose, nose, 142.
Nothing-at-all, 93.
Now I lay me down to sleep, 17.
Now what do you think, 143.

O all you little blackey tops, 60.
O dear, what can the matter be? 187.
O the little rusty dusty miller, 125.
Of a little take a little, 115.
Of all the sayings in this world, 116.
Oh, mother, I shall be married to Mr. Punchinello, 138.
Oh, rare Harry Parry, 86.
Oh that I were, 135.
Oh, the brave old Duke of York, 62.
Oh, what have you got for dinner, Mrs. Bond? 171.
Oh where, oh where has my little dog gone? 70.

There was a man lived in the moon, 162–3.
There was a man of double deed, 136.
There was a man of Thessaly, 140.
There was a man rode through our town, 154.
There was a man who had no eyes, 154.
There was a monkey climbed a tree, 144.
There was a piper had a cow, 141.
There was a rat, for want of stairs, 140.
There was a thing a full month old, 153.
There was a wee bit wifie, 45.
There was an old crow, 141.
There was an old man, and he had a calf, 144.
There was an old man in a velvet coat, 93.
There was an old man who lived in Middle Row, 96.
There was an old woman and nothing she had, 137.
There was an old woman and what do you think? 139.
There was an old woman called Nothing-at-all, 93.
There was an old woman had three cows, 66.
There was an old woman, her name was Peg, 93.
There was an old woman lived under a hill, 94, 140.
There was an old woman sat spinning, 138.
There was an old woman sold puddings and pies, 87.
There was an old woman tossed up in a basket, 70.
There was an old woman who lived in a shoe, 45.
There was an old woman who lived in Dundee, 84.
There was an owl lived in an oak, 67.
There were three cooks of Colebrook, 102.
There were three jovial Welshmen, 161.
There were three sisters in a hall, 155.
There were two birds sat on a stone, 71.
There were two wrens upon a tree, 51.
Thirty days hath September, 112.
Thirty white horses, 151.
This is the house that Jack built, 47–49.
This is the key of the kingdom, 125.
This is the way the ladies ride, 14.
This is Willy Walker, and that's Tam Sim, 16.
This little pig had a rub-a-dub, 5.
This little pig went to market, 5.
This pig got in the barn, 5.
This year, next year, 110.
Three Acres of Land, 188.
Three blind mice, see how they run! 63.
Three Brethren from Spain, 206.
Three children sliding on the ice, 139.
Three crooked cripples went through Crip-plegate, 156.
Three grey geese in a green field grazing, 156.

Three Jovial Welshmen, 161.
Three little ghostesses, 92.
Three little kittens, 65.
Three Ships, 204.
Three wise men of Gotham, 82.
Three young rats with black felt hats, 39.
Through storm and wind, 118.
Thumb bold, 4.
Thumb he, 4.
Thumbikin, Thumbikin, broke the barn, 4.
Thumbkin says, I'll dance, 4.
Thumpaty, thumpaty, thump, *see* 174.
Tickly, tickly, on your knee, 7.
Tiddle liddle lightum, 54.
Timothy Titus took two ties, 158.
Tinker, tailor, 110.
Tit, tat, toe, 26.
Titty cum tawtay, 77.
To make your candles last for aye, 116.
To market, to market, 12.
To sleep easy all night, 114.
Toe Tipe, 5.
Toe, trip and go, 3.
Tom Brown's two little Indian boys, 86.
Tom, he was a piper's son, 164–5.
Tom Thumbkin, 4.
Tom Thumb's Picture Alphabet, 106–7.
Tom Tinker's Dog, 41.
Tom, Tom, the piper's son, 46.
Tommy kept a chandler's shop, 38.
Tommy O'Linn was a Scotsman born, 202.
Tommy Snooks and Bessy Brooks, *see* 33.
Tommy Tacket, 99.
Tommy Tibule, 5.
Tommy Tittlemouse, 27.
Tommy Trot, a man of law, 98.
Tommy Tucker, 44.
Tragical Death of A, Apple Pie, 108–9.
Trip upon trenchers, and dance upon dishes, 177.
Trit trot to market to buy a penny doll, 13.
Tweedledum and Tweedledee, 40.
Twelve Days of Christmas, 198–9.
Twelve pears hanging high, 155.
Twinkle, twinkle, little star, 36.
Twist about, turn about, 63.
Two bodies have I, 148.
Two brothers we are, 149.
Two legs sat upon three legs, 151.
Two little dicky birds, 9.
Two little dogs, 34.

Up and down the City Road, 71.
Up at Piccadilly oh! 59.
Up hill and down dale, 83.
Up street and down street, 122.
Up the wooden hill to Bedfordshire, 17.
Upon a cock-horse to market I'll trot, 12.
Upon Paul's steeple stands a tree, 137.

Wag a leg, wag a leg, 16.
Warm hands, warm, 53.

INDEX OF FIRST LINES

F   for   Finny
I   for   Inny
N   for   Nicklebrandy
I   for   Isaac painter's wife
S   for   Sugar candy.